CW00687610

EL BANDITO
ORIG WILLIAMS
THE AUTOBIOGRAPHY

EL BANDITO
ORIG WILLIAMS
THE AUTOBIOGRAPHY

with Martyn Williams

To Wendy and Tara

First impression: 2010

Cover photos: Gerallt Llewelyn & Roger G Brown
Cover design: Alan Thomas

ISBN: 978 184771 292 9

Printed on acid-free and partly recycled paper
and published and bound in Wales by
Y Lolfa Cyf., Talybont, Ceredigion SY24 5HE
e-mail ylolfa@ylolfa.com
website www.ylolfa.com
tel 01970 832 304
fax 832 782

Acknowledgements

THIS BOOK HAS BEEN long in the making. The success of Orig's Welsh-language book *Cario'r Ddraig*, superbly chronicled by Myrddin ap Dafydd, prompted Orig to think of an English version. His tales, he convinced me, needed to be told!

So we sat down in Llansannan, Cardiff Bay and a few pubs along the way and recorded and talked about what he thought could be published! Those were always lively discussions.

This is it.

So I wish to thank, in no particular order, other than immediately placing Wendy and Tara at the top of the list, all the wrestlers who have been more than willing to collect their thoughts, and in particular Peter Nulty, Brian Dixon and Mitzi, Mighty John Quinn, Dave Finlay Snr and Klondyke Kate for helping me trace a few addresses and numbers.

Thanks also to: Vanessa Toulmin at University of Sheffield's National Fairground Archive; the photographers – Gerallt Llewelyn, Jeff Wilde and Peter Nulty, and the encouragement from the lads at www.wrestlingheritage.co.uk.

We had hoped to attract support from the Welsh Books Council for this publication, but as Orig would say "you know what FA stands for? – Football Association!"

Things are a bit quieter in Wales since his passing.

Martyn Williams

Foreword

THERE IS NOT A day that goes past when I don't think of Orig Williams. Whatever sparks that off – a remark, a situation, or something in the ring or gym – I think about the man who took me on board. I owe everything to him. He fixed me up to become Goliath in *Gladiators*; he sought my introduction to World Wrestling Entertainment (WWE) and he became a 'second father' to me, if that makes sense. It certainly will, to many in the game.

Mind you, that didn't stop him from giving me a daily bollocking. That was his way – uncompromising, energetic, but always honest. He told it like it was and in extremely colourful languages – sometimes English or Anglo-Saxon, but more often than not to me, in Welsh. Orig always had a burning ambition to produce a Welsh-speaking wrestling champion, and he never tired in his search for a potential candidate.

Personally, I had no more than a passive interest in wrestling – other than watching it on the TV occasionally. But one night, the Orig road show came to my home town of Porthmadog in north Wales. I had obviously heard of Orig before, since he was something of a legend in north Wales, but I had never met him. I soon realised that this man was larger than life.

He strutted and strolled around the ring, telling us how evil that night's 'heel' was, and why the 'heel' deserved the ultimate punishment – and he was the referee! It was all hugely entertaining and Orig had an enormous talent for engaging his audiences. I was transfixed by the show, but was too shy to introduce myself. Fortunately, one of my mates, a little worse for drink, had no such inhibitions. So we ended up having a chat. My height must have impressed him, and he must have thought I had some potential as next morning he was on the phone. He invited me to Rhyl and to a training school run by Brian Dixon at Birkenhead – another stalwart and major influence who would become a great friend. Until then, I had been working for the family carpentry and funeral director business in Tremadog. Orig would not take no for an answer. I was on my way.

That was the beginning. In my first year with him I must have done fifty shows, and every day was a learning experience and a valuable education. By now he had his 'Welsh project', and it was as much as I could do to prevent him challenging anyone he came across. For example, he wanted a double-page spread in the *Daily Post* with a headline, "Welsh rugby players are a bunch of 'Big Babies' compared to his men", just to create a stir, and publicity for our shows.

I have two regrets. The first is that I only knew the man for some five years – I wish it had been thirty. I also regret that I do not have a photograph of him and me together. In all those shows we did, especially in Ireland, not one photographer took a snap of me with the man I hold in such high esteem.

Before he left us, he knew that I had signed to go to wrestle in the United States. It gives me great comfort to know that that is what he wanted. But prior to that opportunity, I also know he was still organising tours and shows, right up to a few weeks before his final count. We'd been to Ireland, but the crowds were small, but he kept on going. I knew that he was losing money at these shows, but to Orig, wrestling, and the deals to be made was his life, and nothing else mattered more – apart from Wendy and Tara.

He had his catch phrases... "Saturday night is fight night", or "there are fighters and drinkers – and I love both".

I doubt if we shall ever see another Orig Williams. I just wish I had that photograph!

Barri Griffiths
Goliath in *Gladiators*
Mason Ryan in WWE

Introduction

Allah Madhat... Allah Madhat
[Let Allah give you strength]
Aki... Aki... Aki
INFIDEL... INFIDEL... INFIDEL

THE SO-CALLED 'ENDEARING' CHANTS of welcome to a proud Welshman – carrying a small flag of a dragon, in Pakistan. This welcome was provided by a chorus of 100,000 excited Pakistani wrestling supporters who hated my guts! Not because I was Welsh, but because I was white and British. The location was Lahore Cricket ground, with every seat and viewing point occupied. They were not there for the cricket – they were there to see the British atone for so many things in the past. They wanted to see blood being spilt – mine.

This was a common salutation to those confronting the Muslim world and I must say it was quite convincing when chanted by 100,000 wrestling supporters. Was I frightened? You bet! I was not the subject of their good wishes, nor was Allah being asked to grant me any special consideration. Not a single white-toothed, white-eyed supporter extended me any friendly wishes. "*Infidel... Infidel... Infidel*", they hissed and shouted. To them, I represented the oppressor and intruder. They would offer no mercy to a Brit with their relentless chanting. But I wasn't a Brit, for God's sake! And where was my Welsh Calvinistic Methodist God, the one and only God according to my Sunday school teacher? Having a night off, I assumed. Wise God!

Retreat or withdrawal from the ring was not an option. I would have been trampled alive. What on earth was I doing here, drowning in a sea of hatred? There was no escape route. The entrance of my opponent Akram Bholu into the test cricket ground (an adapted wrestling stadium for that night) had been greeted by 100,000 decibels, or so it seemed.

Shirts, towels, flags and scarves were flung into the night sky, to be followed by a mighty roar of approval. He was undefeated, a legend, a God. Had I not been told? So what imbecile of a Welshman had accepted such a challenge? My bowels were beginning to react – too late. Trapped! The sweat poured, and I began to fear for my life.

Akram walked in draped in the Pakistan flag and waved to the crowd. To the frenzied mob he was a hero, a leader, and was close to Allah in his personal quest for immortality. I was a mere brief interruption. Another huge roar came from the crowd who stood on chairs or perched in trees, on roofs and ladders. He orchestrated the crowd, but there was no need.

They had been his ever since the fight had been announced. Whatever the British had inflicted upon Pakistan in those bygone days was about to be avenged. There was no sense in telling them that I wasn't a Brit after all, but a boy from the Welsh hills. Whatever cowardly thoughts entered my head (and there were quite a few) had to be conquered. But that was impossible as Akram waved again to the crowd who were now almost salivating at the thought of a limb-by-limb destruction of the infidel.

Not an eye was cast in my direction. I shut my eyes and thought of home: green grass, sheep grazing, the river Conwy, the village square and the tranquillity of Ysbyty Ifan, my birthplace in the Welsh hills. *"Allah Madhat... Allah Madhat"*. The din of 100,000 frantic Pakistanis shattered whatever tranquil thoughts I had. This was indeed a very long way from the little village of Ysbyty Ifan.

CHAPTER 1

Ysbyty Ifan

I COULD NEVER HAVE been an upstanding member of the Ysbyty Ifan community. My destiny was hewn in the past. I would dare to be different. Our village, in a north-east Wales rural valley, had a marvellous sinister part in history. Not the stuff of comics, make-believe or legends, this was for real.

The Crusader warrior knights and monks of St John of Jerusalem had established a hospice (*ysbyty* in Welsh) on the site of the present church. It was a sanctuary for travellers caught up in the countless feuds and conflicts between the Welsh and the English. As the knights lost control of their estates, Ysbyty Ifan grew into a notorious lawless haven for thieves, murderers, pirates and outlaws, where only the meanest and most ruthless survived. As time went by, they were all hunted down and killed by Henry VII's lawman Meredydd ab Ieuan.

The mountains had also been home to the infamous Red Bandit gang, the *Gwylliaid Cochion*, a vicious group of murderers and plunderers. They had been supporters of Owain Glyndŵr, prince of Wales, and after his defeat had fled to the hills to seek protection. These were peasants whose weapons were primitive farming tools. They hid in the woods and were ruthless. Large areas and estates were controlled by these red-haired bandits. When caught, they were hanged.

Therefore, imagine the impression of such tales on the boys of our village square, kneeling wide-eyed and motionless, as old men told and re-told, with more than a twinkle in their eyes, the ruthless and lawless exploits of our forefathers. "Thieves, cheats and liars, that is what we were," they said and I have never doubted that the indoctrination on the village square was to prepare me well for the journey ahead.

The village may have been less unruly by the time I sat and joined the 'university' of the square. At that time, my village was a television, computer, CD, mobile and fax free area; conversations spoke only of strength, endurance and courage. Local men with strength were heroes. In a world where man and beast fought daily against the mountainous terrain for a sparse return, the weak and meek would not survive – nor were they respected. There were countless challenges (such as lifting and carrying competitions) between the sons of farms, villages and valleys. This was our sort of entertainment; these were our sort of challenges.

Fights were commonplace, and those who won walked tall, since that was the simple way of earning respect in a community so very down to earth. Chapel people talked about them, but turned a blind eye to the physical confrontations. It was not of their world. They took no pity on those who fisted their way through life, and they treated them as if they were untouchables.

The people of the mountain land and its farms were hard, rugged, with faces gouged by work and gritted by weather. They were resourceful, independent, sombre, strangely shy and extremely Welsh. Few spoke English, and those that did had few listeners. Not for them the niceties of towns and cities. They had heard of them: London, Liverpool and Chester – even talked, read and wondered about them, but those places had little to do with Ysbyty Ifan. Those were the dwellings of wealthy English people, or those who had moved away.

We had wealth which you could not buy.

The rushing River Conwy dissected the village as it raced towards the castles of despised English kings and the coast of north Wales. It could be a fierce river, but the only reason that a bridge was built was when one of the village women drowned after slipping on the original stepping stones. The river was also a county boundary line.

I lived in Denbighshire, but fetched water from Caernarfonshire. Imagine the pride and stigma when we, on the Denbighshire side, were given our own water tap. Even better the invention of a local man, Thomas John Roberts, who managed to create a home-made generator – enough power for a flickering light bulb in each of Ysbyty Ifan's cottages. Our village may have been dimly lit, but our neighbouring villages flickered in candlelight and oil lamps. We never tired of telling them that they were still in the dark ages! Mr Roberts's invention was enough to power a wireless as well – with entry into a whole new fascinating world of news, words, places, images and heroes.

A chapel, church, mill, forge, school, hall, four small shops, a communal water pump, pub and square, all encroached by two-up, two-down cottages with a toilet in the garden – that was Ysbyty Ifan. What more could you want? The square was everything. A place to moan and to mourn, to console and celebrate, to talk and to listen, to castigate and to court, and for us, hobnailed-boot young sportsmen, it was Highbury, Anfield and Madison Square Gardens all rolled into one.

"Spitting what?" "Spitting Evans?" Time and time again I was asked to explain where I was from, and time and time again, the Anglo-Saxon ear could not comprehend. I would attempt some new-found English phrases. Eventually patience – not one of my great redeeming strengths in life – was exhausted.

"Listen, mate, let me tell you about Ysbyty Ifan. A few miles up the single-track mountain road from Ysbyty Ifan are the pearly gates of Heaven. You can see them from the mountain on a clear night. It would do you well to come for a familiarisation visit before the grim reaper calls."

Few might have believed me, but at least it was a way of explaining the beginning of my journey, and possibly the end of theirs.

What I couldn't comprehend, much later, was that a vast number of people had not heard of my beloved Wales, let alone Ysbyty Ifan. Far better, I told myself, to be called a 'Welsh bastard' than a 'sheep shagger' – at least they recognised my nationality. I did my bit as Ysbyty Ifan's unpaid tourism officer.

There were no airs and graces in Ysbyty Ifan. No one could afford them, even if they knew what they were. My uncle, Lewis Williams, was the urine collector. Bucket in hand he would call on the houses to collect female urine, "full of ammonia you see", for wool washing. "Red heads are best," he would tell us, but never explained why. Another uncle went off to Patagonia in Argentina to teach Welsh, which was viewed by all as being very brave and honourable. Better than a piss collector anyway.

Everything was shared – misery, merriment, poverty and pewters, tales and sometimes truths. Our home was a stone-built, slate-roofed terraced house, grim to the eye, spotless inside and home to my father, mother and me. My father came from another planet: a village called Trefriw, some fourteen miles away, and wasn't really accepted as a 'Sbyty man' for years. He kept his own counsel, worked in the neighbouring quarries, scarcely raised his voice, except when talking enthusiastically about hard men and boxers from south Wales, an area he'd been employed in at one time before returning after only three weeks. He told me of prize fighters, bare-knuckle fighters, boxing booths and champions, but always when he was sure my mother was elsewhere and out of hearing.

Mother accepted his weekly money, and went about her business cleaning the school and chapel. They were both devout chapel-goers and it was a place that I was to frequent in my Sunday-best clothes at least five times a week and three times on a Sunday. It was a place where I experienced fear... the moment I saw him.

His name was the Reverend William Pritchard. A large, dark-haired man with anger in his voice and venom in the sermons directed to all who sinned – or thought about sinning. We were castigated to hell on a weekly basis. With his resonant, carrying voice, he put the fear of God into his flock, and a few grazing flocks outside as well. People would not visit his house, just in case he was practising his malevolent sermons. His flock would silently leave eggs, bread and milk outside his front door and slip away. These were donations to ensure acceptance into heaven, rather than to the 'other place'.

We were all in awe of the Reverend Pritchard. He was not to be questioned, and many a time I would look at crestfallen sinners in their pews. Black-suited and black-laced with stiff, white collars – petrified mortals. The village pump would cleanse linen; the chapel would cleanse souls.

There were sinners. Better to move out if you became an unmarried mother in Ysbyty Ifan. The only pub had two customers, one from one end of the village, the other from the opposite end. Little wonder it closed. However, it didn't stop the Saturday night bus to the bright lights and pubs of nearby Llanrwst being filled with revellers. But you didn't sin on your doorstep. Hangover sinners humbly waited to be lambasted on Sunday mornings, by the Reverend Pritchard.

Outside the chapel, it was a different world and a mischievous one. My world! The custom for us youngsters was to recite a biblical verse each Sunday morning in front of the hell-bound gathering, and woe betide you if you failed the Reverend, your mother and father and the rest of Ysbyty Ifan. Once, however, I forgot to learn the verse on a Saturday night, and so the boys on the square gave me an alternative. "Our cat has been humping next door's" was a quick one to learn, they said. And I did. However, something told me that it wasn't quite right, and when the Reverend beckoned that it was my turn to recite my verse, I froze and said nothing, which was probably a worse sin. The row I received from my mother at home is a vivid memory. I never spoke again to the Reverend after that incident.

If I failed to absorb the pulpit's lessons, the square was very different. Here you would find a few men who had travelled outside the village and had seen mighty and wonderful things. Some had sailed with the merchant navy, some had been to the coalmines of south Wales like my father and some had even seen Ted Drake and Eddie Hapgood play for Arsenal. We sat and listened to those who had been to wonderful places and to those who repeated these stories thinking they had. This was a vocal and oral library of truths, half-truths and lies. Sunday's truth was so different from the weekday version.

Very few of the storytellers, whether they were farmers or quarrymen, had received any schooling beyond the 3Rs. Yet the quarrymen would discuss poetry and ideas after their shifts, and the farmers would have been taught the biblical way. They were princely storytellers, painters of words, observers of life, rural philosophers – and they had an attentive following.

Their young audience absorbed everything. Footballers were legends, but men with strength, like the boxers from south Wales, were gods. Beating a man with power, strength and skill was the ultimate in terms of Ysbyty Ifan recognition. We understood that if you could beat a man or carry more than the man next to you, this was the ladder of promotion and relegation. Nothing else mattered. Was not Ysbyty Ifan a fortress of strength, of independent Welshness protected by hard and strong men? Was not Rhys Gethin, the right-hand man of the great Welsh prince and warrior Owain Glyndŵr, from Ysbyty Ifan? The 'school' of the square had no better pupil than me.

I became obsessed with physical challenges. I ran wherever I went – sometimes for miles. I was Eddie Hapgood, the Arsenal defender, and Norman, my mate from Number 5, was Ted Drake in the three-a-side daily FA Cup final on the square. "Nothing good will come of that boy," said a relative to my mother, "best he become a reverend". If there was a game to be had, a challenge to be met, I was there, and there to win, not merely to take part. Most of the boys at school helped out with farm duties and shied away from 'kicking air' as they put it. Farming was not for me, especially since the local colonel, the only titled man in the village, apart from the church minister, turned me down for a job. People shook their heads and muttered as I ran past. I knew what they were saying. I had no future.

Sport was everything to me. Sunday papers were not allowed in our home. "You can read the same news in the Monday paper," my aunt would say, but a friend and neighbour did have the *Empire News* delivered. I couldn't wait to read the sports pages and I devoured them. Here were my heroes in print, and it was here that I read extracts from the legendary Tommy Farr's biography. My father and all the pundits from the square had told me how Farr had been robbed of the boxing world heavyweight title by Joe Louis after fifteen gruelling rounds in a far away place called New York. Who was I to disbelieve the impartial expertise of the square?

Farr, Freddie Welsh, Jimmy Wilde and Jim Driscoll were gods. They had achieved boxing fame on both sides of the Atlantic and they were all Welsh, albeit from south Wales. How I wished to emulate them. How I envied the south for producing such men. Farr wrote, "I am no angel. There are no angels in Tonypandy, nor yet in all the coalfields of my native Wales." These words were to inspire me for a lifetime! I was destined to become no angel.

The Farr stories and the *Empire News* sports' coverage had another enthusiast and local reader. Dewi Rees, my teacher at Llanrwst Grammar School, which I was to attend after leaving the 'university' of the square, was to become my sports mentor. Although he was Welsh, he had an unfamiliar accent, so he was treated with suspicion and respect. He knew his sport and that was OK by me.

Here was a man who guided me towards a career in sport, and football in particular. He recognised early on that apart from a love of reading Welsh literature and poetry, I was destined, as he told a smirking classroom, to become a bus driver – certainly not an academic. Life was too short to spend in libraries when there were football pitches outside.

But, suddenly, our entire world, or the world of Ysbyty Ifan, was shattered. The Second World War reached Ysbyty Ifan, which was unusual, as most things seemed to pass us by completely. We were aware of a world outside, but only just. The war arrived with vengeance, and we were ill-prepared. We could not understand what this war had to do with Ysbyty Ifan. This war was all to do with people in London and England, not with Wales and our village. Hitler could not have heard of Ysbyty Ifan. But the war came nonetheless. Soldiers arrived with their anti aircraft-guns and huge lamps. We couldn't work out why Ysbyty Ifan had become one of Churchill's priorities. How had he heard of us?

The soldiers, who were billeted in the village hall during the day, took to the mountain at night to look at Hitler's bombing raids on Liverpool and seek out enemy aircraft with their searchlights. At first there was fascination, but then came resentment. Why had we been dragged from our rural and Welsh tranquillity into something that was none of our doing? That resentment was enforced when one of the soldiers left a coat on the village hall boiler and the entire building was burnt to ashes.

The soldiers spoke English, which few of us understood. There were some who said that putting up with the soldiers was our part in the war effort. Then, when a plane on its way back to Germany dropped a bomb on the mountain, there was genuine fear that Hitler, having found Liverpool, had now discovered Ysbyty Ifan. The soldiers kept to themselves, and we played football on our own.

Worse was to follow. Churchill changed the clock by two hours but failed to tell the local dawn chorus and the cows which had to be milked. Nor had he consulted the inhabitants of Ysbyty Ifan. This was interpreted as an intrusive act of English boorish behaviour which was much despised, resulting in Ysbyty Ifan retaining its original time and telling Churchill to go to hell. Of course, it resulted in chaos. The buses from the 'outside world' were on Churchill's time. So too were wireless sets, deliveries and bombing raids, and often the question was asked, "Is that Churchill's time, or ours?"

Then, for us youngsters came the most threatening development of all – worse than the ration books and the men who begrudgingly had to leave to fight for their king and country. The evacuees from Liverpool's Scotland Road invaded our territory. They were not like us at all. Some took pity on them, some saw them as yet another of Churchill's intrusions. They had not seen a cow, sheep or goat in their entire lives. But with them came girls – attractive ones too. Sylvia was my favourite, and I invited her to one of the highlights of the Ysbyty Ifan calendar – the visit of the stallion to the forge to cover the local mares. When she realised what was involved, the brief courtship ended with Sylvia calling me a dirty Welsh bastard.

The evacuees were also billeted to homes and farms, and linguistically and culturally they were outcasts. They spoke no Welsh, and so couldn't understand us. They kept to themselves or made friends with the soldiers. A little later, another invasion of Italian prisoners of war came to work on the fields. They spoke no English, but they could play football. A far better relationship was formed with the Italians than the moaning evacuees.

It all came to a head on a summer's afternoon. The local

lads, especially the farm labourers, would hold informal boxing matches in front of the forge. No ring, no bell, no rounds, no referee – only gloves and reputations to be made or lost. A match – or mismatch I thought – was made between me and one of the evacuees, Edwin Flynn. My promoter, manager and the next boxer on the tarmac ring was Aled Lloyd – home on a fortnight's leave from the RAF. Aled, six foot tall and fifteen stone, was something of a local hero. His son, Terry Lloyd, became a war correspondent for ITN and was tragically killed in Iraq. Aled, lacing my gloves turned to me and said in Welsh, "Do your best. Just remember what I have told you – left, left, left and then right." Edwin Flynn was fifteen years old, and I was thirteen. He was three inches taller and a stone heavier. Aled had already told him to take it easy since I was younger and smaller. "Go," came the command.

My mouth was dry. I was petrified. I certainly wasn't prepared for the ferocity of Flynn's opening barrage of blows. This was taking it easy? Down I went, and I was forced to look at his ugly gloating face. "Come on sheep shagger!" he shouted. I got up and wiped the loose chippings from my gloves and decided to use Aled's plan of attack with three lefts and a right. Unfortunately, only one of them found its target. "Is that all you've got you Welsh sheep shagger?"

Aled told him to shut up. I was now in a rage and charged towards him with windmill fists, but to no avail, and I promptly walked into a well-aimed upper cut. Down I went on one knee as Aled told me to get up and wipe the chippings from the gloves. In came Flynn again, with a barrage of blows, which left me floundering on all fours. I was being pulverised and Edwin Flynn was teaching me an English lesson that I was never to forget. I knew I was running out of energy and would not last much more.

"Wipe your gloves," said Aled. But I faked it. My gloves were laced with wet chippings. In came Flynn for the finish. I stepped back a few paces, and with all my might I landed a haymaker between his eyes. "Agghhaa!" he screamed as he went down, sprawled on the floor clutching his face, with blood streaming everywhere. "Who is the sheep shagger now?" I shouted at him.

"You are, you Welsh bastard. You had chippings on your gloves."
His lips were already swelling.

The watching crowd quietly approved. Most of them were local,
and some had fought earlier. It would not have done to be beaten
by the evacuee in front of this lot. I was delighted, chippings or
no chippings. News of the fight went round the village. Had I
cheated? Yes, of course. Had I won and scored one for Ysbyty
Ifan? Yes, I had, and it mattered. It was the first time I had been
forced into using dubious tactics, but it would not be the last.

On Sunday I walked in front of my mother as we headed
for chapel, giving all and sundry sight of my cuts and bruises.
In a village where strength and determination was noted and
recorded, this was my first walk of glory. It was a good feeling.
For the sinners that day in chapel, the sermon was based on 'My
cup runneth over'. Little did the Reverend realise how apt that
sermon was for the young, growing sinner in front of him.

If those soldiers had not set our village hall alight, then life
in Ysbyty would have been more tolerable. It was a literate and
musical community, and there was nothing more engaging than
to hear the area's poets compete against each other in verse. We
enjoyed those evenings, and that was probably the inspiration
that made me learn and appreciate so much Welsh poetry. In
addition, I was sent to work, during school holidays, to a local
carpenter and craftsman, Huw Sel. I think he realised quickly
that I had no future in wood, but he was a recognised poet and
ballad writer. What better company – and a friend for life.

Unfortunately, my bent and enthusiasm for the written word
did not extend to other subjects at Llanrwst Grammar School,
other than sporting activity. Soccer and athletics were my forte,
and we'd spend the summer weekends competing at various
village sports days and earning some what was then decent
pocket money.

Some of the older lads were leaving the village, either to work
elsewhere, to sign up for the king's army or to go to college. The
latter was not an option for me. But the innocent life of a growing
young man was coming to an end. I too became conscious that I
would have to leave Ysbyty. That day was fast approaching.

CHAPTER 2

AIRCRAFTSMAN
2449290 Williams O

IF I HAD ANY talents other than sporting ones, they were certainly well hidden. Whereas others at Llanrwst Grammar would become scholars, surgeons and scientists, the only career counselling I can recall was that prophecy of Mr Rees, telling me that I would end up driving a bus around the valley. "Nothing good will come of that boy, him and all his football," was the agreed prediction of Mrs Davies, Mrs Jones and every other Mrs in Ysbyty Ifan.

So, it was inevitable that on leaving the confined comfort of the school, the village and friends that I was destined for the forces and national service. Unfortunately, the Welsh armies of Owain Glyndŵr and Prince Llywellyn had long disappeared, so I couldn't enlist there. I had no real appetite for pledging my allegiance to His Majesty's armed forces. Not I, from the rebellious Celtic fortress of Ysbyty Ifan. For goodness sake, as kids we had been plotting the downfall of England in our dreams, games and village square conversations for the best part of a decade. The Racecourse in Wrexham, Ninian Park in Cardiff and the Vetch Field in Swansea were our Wembleys. Our heroes were Meredith, Wally Barnes, Tommy Farr, Jimmy Wilde, Jim Driscoll and Trevor Ford. The English had double-barrelled names, whereas we had double-barrelled-chested proud Welshmen.

My future alternatives? The navy meant going to sea. The army promised a short life. So, my only option was the RAF, and my destination and base for the next eighteen months would be Padgate near Warrington. My fears of being isolated in a foreign land were justified, but I was not prepared for the humiliation.

Within hours of my arrival I was shaven bald by a man with a one-speed mechanical shearing machine, then kitted out in an ill-fitting uniform and called a 'mountain goat' and a 'caveman' by everyone at the camp above my rank... that was about 5,000 of them.

Our corporal had taken an instant dislike to me and the feeling was mutual. I suspect that I wasn't being singled out for verbal abuse, but it certainly felt like it. This was especially true when we began six weeks of square-bashing. Hardly a woken hour would pass without marching, with our corporal waxing lyrical at our inadequacies, sexuality, aptitude and attitude. Being Welsh I was picked upon because I would often mutter something in Welsh, which he would want repeated – and that would really set him off. 'Mountain goats' are not bilingual – but this one was!

So here I was, bald and kitted out and in an RAF uniform. Not that you would have known that it was the Royal Air Force. Padgate only had one plane, and that was the ornamental spitfire on the front gates! The only respite from all that mind-numbing marching was the assault course – no problem for a 'mountain goat' from Ysbyty Ifan.

Suddenly, I was summoned! What had I done? I was marched to the camp's headquarters, to be met by Wing Commander Young DFC. I gave him a massive salute, expecting some sort of punishment for a crime that for the life of me I couldn't remember.

"Stand at ease, Williams," said the highly decorated man.

"How would you like to become aircrew?" he asked.

I was dumbfounded, and it took me some time to gather my thoughts. The invitation was an honour, although every wartime film I had seen involving RAF aircrews had usually ended up with them being shot down. But this was 1949 and the war was over. So what did aircrew mean? I certainly did not want to be a tail-gunner, watching the world go by with your back to it.

"Why me, sir?" I blurted.

"Do not question your superior officer, Williams," he replied.

"That's it," I thought, "I've blown it. There will be a charge for that."

"I will tell you, Williams," he said, "you are only one of three people on this camp with PULHEEMS 1."

Whatever that was I didn't have a clue. Since there were only three of us suffering from whatever it was, it clearly wasn't contagious. But I wasn't about to ask, just in case he'd give me another reprimand. Thankfully, he must have realised my dilemma.

"Let me explain Williams what PULHEEMS means," he said. "Every man here is assessed as to his physical condition, and the letters PULHEEMS stand for Physique – Upper Limbs – Lower Limbs – Hearing – Eyes Left and Right – Mentality and Stability. You, Williams, have scored top marks in every category, which means that you are PULHEEMS 1. That makes you eligible for air crew. Do I make myself clear Williams?"

"Yes, sir," I replied. Three bags full, I was not on a charge!

"And your response?" he asked.

I asked him if I could consider the issue for twenty-four hours. The cheek of it!

Back at our quarters, I was not short of advice from my fellow square-bashers. They did a job on me, "Become an aircrew member? You must have left your brains and balls on those mountains." I was quite proud of my PULHEEMS, now that I understood what it meant. But then, the killer blow. "What's the point of being the fittest, most stable and best physical specimen around here, if they only want a rear-gunner?" asked one of my learned colleagues.

That did it! All those war films came back to me, and I gave the wing commander my decision – politely of course! He thought I was insane. At least I wasn't in trouble – for the time being. After six weeks of marching – and what a bore that was – along came a twenty-four hours pass. Twenty-four glorious hours of what could loosely be called freedom. I knew I couldn't make it back to Ysbyty Ifan. By the time I would have got there I would have to wave goodbye and return.

I had a plan. I had met a girl who used to come on holiday to our village and we had kept in touch, despite taking her to see the local mare being covered by a visiting stallion. She was a 'looker' and we'd enjoyed some innocent romps in the hay. It didn't take me long to pluck up the courage to write and ask her for a date during my twenty-four hours. Sylvia lived in Liverpool, so off I went in my His Majesty's RAF uniform and we met at Lime Street Station and found a cinema. I have no idea what the film was and I doubt whether she had time to watch much of it either. Alas, on leaving the pictures I was collared by an RAF on-duty policeman. I had not replaced my beret on leaving the cinema – a most hideous crime and reason to be charged with disgracing the king's uniform. A bloody beret!

I was put on charge and given a six-day Confined to Barracks (CB) sentence, which meant reporting in full gear with a backpack every four hours to the duty room. And woes betide you if there was a hair or lace out of place. Few served the minimum sentence period and I was no exception. I served my CB for twelve days. PULHEEMS indeed!

The RAF did have one redeeming feature – sport. Little did I know that joining the RAF would be the defining moment for my development as a soccer player. However, it did not begin too promisingly. About a hundred of us were on parade when an incredibly loud corporal asked for eleven volunteers. Not a soul moved. He then asked if there were any us who thought we could play football. The response was astonishing. Just about everybody fancied himself as God's gift to football. So the corporal set about asking a few of them for their credentials and experience at previous clubs.

I could not believe that of the fifty or so who had held their hands aloft, many had played for Arsenal, Liverpool or Spurs. What a talented bunch! And when I offered my credential as being a Llanrwst Grammar School player – the corporal had the audacity to say he'd not heard of it! So, against the might of Anfield, Highbury and White Hart Lane, I was to be thrown into a trial game. It did not take long to realise that the closest my colleagues had come to the colours of their famous clubs was eating a pasty outside the grounds.

The camp organised a tournament between some fifteen teams and our lot reached the final where we were scheduled to meet our masters, the physical education officers – and some of them had good football pedigrees. We lost the game narrowly, but having scored two goals against my superiors I must have made an impression. The next day I was asked if I would like to stay on at Padgate for the remainder of my national service, which had now been extended to two years by the British Government.

And, although, I would have preferred going to RAF Valley on Anglesey, which was slightly nearer to home, I was not opposed to staying on at Padgate since I was earning my spurs and respect on the football field. I could easily have been sent to Scotland or Germany – just for once, I was happy to stay in England! They gave me an undemanding job as a clerk in the health department, which meant in reality that I could train and play as much as I wanted. The gym was a favourite place, for football, basketball and boxing – this RAF life was turning out to be quite tolerable!

But clouds were gathering, and they were none of my making. There were a few thousand of us at Padgate and across town, in a place called Burtonwood, the US forces had their base of 2,000 men. They were 'over here' all right, with their allowances much better than ours – and very much louder. The local council in Warrington had given planning permission for a girls' college to be built just outside the Padgate entrance. What vision! So, we had 200 available females on our doorstep – for 5,000 males. Not quite parity, and the Americans were on the hunt as well, with their chocolate, nylons and bullshit. Inevitably, this situation was going to result in trouble.

Every Saturday night became fight night in downtown Warrington. You had no choice but to defend your honour, or someone else's. The usual venue was a pub called the Seven Seas, but you wouldn't enter unless you were prepared to fight for your country, your mate, his mate – and I did my best for all kinds of mates that I'd never even met. It was mainly between us and them – the Yanks – and you would not have thought we had just fought a world war alongside them. When it all got out of hand, the military authorities decided to do something about it.

Since most of the officers were from the double-barrelled public school sector, it didn't surprise us to hear that the 'toffs' had organised competitions between the two camps. They proposed a game of baseball, which naturally the Yanks won, then a game of rugby, which we won in a marvellously bloody battle, but their third proposition was a boxing contest. Aha! Now this was of interest. But as ever, there were complications. The Yanks didn't have a featherweight, and we didn't have a heavyweight. Some brigadier somewhere suggested a compromise, as brigadiers do. The Yanks would find a featherweight somehow, as long as 'Tommie' found a heavyweight.

"You're our heavyweight, Taff," said a ginger-haired corporal.

"But I am only twelve stone two pounds – five pounds lighter than the minimum weight," I protested – to no avail of course.

"You're the heaviest we've got," he replied.

Eight bouts were to be fought, the maximum number in weight divisions in those days, but after a promising start as a team, we were later being belted. By the time the so-called 'battle of the heavies' approached, the game was over. Then I saw my opponent.

They must have scoured Mississippi, Missouri and Manhattan and flown this one in, I thought. He was taller, bigger and about two and a half stone heavier than me. I cursed the RAF, the brigadier and all the corporals. He was undoubtedly the largest menace I had ever faced. He was a giant, black and very intimidating. I had not met many like him in Ysbyty Ifan.

The bell rang for the first round, the first of three. For a while I comforted myself in the knowledge that I was faster on my feet than the monster in front of me. It was misplaced confidence. In the second round he caught me with a stunning punch to the head, and the boards creaked under my falling weight. As soon as I was up, I was felled again. And then again, and then, thankfully, the bell went.

I was angry and I wasn't quite sure where I was. These had been severe blows from a man who knew how to throw them. By the time the bell went for the final round I had lost it. In he came again, and down I went. The count went to seven. I had had enough. Somehow I got to my feet, when all around appeared to be black. I lunged forward and managed to get my arms around, and pushed him to the ropes. The referee kept shouting, "Break! Break!" But I wasn't listening. Eventually with my opponent tangled up in the ropes, the referee pulled us apart. But I was not done.

As soon as I had the freedom, I kneed the American with all available strength, right in his crotch. He went down like a sunken trawler with a huge groan. The place went mad! "You're disqualified, you disgraceful Welshman," shouted the referee.

"Christ, Taff," screamed my second, "are you completely insane? You'll be put on a charge for that." And I was. But, for that night, I was the toast of Padgate.

Next morning I was standing in front of my station's warrant officer charged with bringing disgrace to the RAF. "Do you have anything to say Williams?" he asked.

"Sir," I said, "I thought it was war." He looked down, then smiled and said,

"I have heard what happened last night, and strictly off the record, you are the kind of man I would like to have on my side. However, I'm afraid you are Confined to Barracks for seven days. Dismiss!"

That un-gentlemanly act against the US forces had ignited a passion in me for more physical confrontation.

Padgate continued to satisfy my sporting and fighting aspirations. If it wasn't by playing football, where I was beginning to make a name for myself, then it was at athletics or in the gym. My friend and fellow runner Bunny Sparks hailed from Manchester, just down the road from the camp. He'd go home every weekend, mainly to go and watch his beloved Manchester United at Old Trafford. When he invited me along for a weekend, I didn't hesitate. We went several times to see United, then skippered by Johnny Carey. That was an education. I marvelled at the skills and the quickness of thought of such players.

But there was more learning to be done. Not only the tuition offered by the sleazy nightclubs of the city, and the even sleazier ladies of the night, but also by Bunny's uncle, who ran a back-alley sweat-room gym for local boxers and wrestlers. I was more enthusiastic about that than being confronted by one of the

Manchester ladies – you'd need a skinful before taking them on!

This was no tiled leisure centre with facilities for all. This was an old warehouse with one light bulb, one ring and mat, and certainly no showers. It was the kind of place you would find up and down the country, the 'centres' of physical activity to scores of generations. It's ironic that with all the facilities our current generations enjoy, we still used to produce more champions from backstreet greasy sweat pits. The hunger isn't there anymore, except in a few.

Johnnie Brown, Bunny's uncle, was a welterweight, and had been around the block a few times. I wasn't quite prepared for the introduction Bunny had in mind, especially on a Sunday morning. "Here's Taff," said Bunny, "he'll go a few rounds with you!" You could tell that Johnnie was a wily character. He was quicker of mind and limb than I was, but I thoroughly enjoyed the experience, though what they would have said about fighting on a Sunday back home in Ysbyty Ifan, I dread to think. Worse was to come. There was also a wrestling mat, and one of the regular guys came over to provoke us. "It doesn't take much to be a boxer, but you need to be a man to be a wrestler," he said.

After decades of the wrestling life, I still remember those words. Strange isn't it? You may argue the point, you might think it all entertainment, but when you get into that ring, there is an element of honour. You can break bones, you are thrown against pillars – but essentially it is all about survival. I'd already seen a bit of wrestling on a rare Sunday day-trip to Llandudno. It was held on a council field, and the fights were between the masked 'Ghoul' and Johnny Mac, with Tommy Jones, a part-time wrestler from Trawsfynydd and a Liverpool docker against Dave Armstrong. It was pretty timid stuff really, but good fun. It must have been deemed suitable entertainment for impressionable school kids as well, since we were taken there by a chapel deacon. So was there anything to this wrestling? In the car on the way back, we were of the opinion that it was a good show, it was all fixed, and that no one could get hurt. We were all learned experts, of course.

The old wrestler beckoned me over to the mat, and he gave me a real introduction to the finer arts. I was down before I could blink and, no matter what I did, he was at least three moves in front of me. It was a fierce and bewildering introduction – but I was fascinated, and when the invitation was made to call in again, weekends became a mixture of Manchester United and grappling with these seasoned campaigners. I was in my element.

At the beginning he was able to pin me down in seconds. But I was taught to block and how to move. I was thrown in against other wrestlers, and they had different moves. So in terms of technique, I knew I was improving. As far as being a wrestler was concerned, there was something else that was required. "You could make a wrestler," he said, "but on the other hand you might not. To be a wrestler, you've got to have something I can't teach you. And that is bottle!"

I have to admit that every return journey to Padgate was a painful one. I was aching in every bone and muscle and in some areas that I didn't even know existed. After the weekends in Manchester, I was forced into submission. This was a tough life! But I had been inspired, not by the sweaty and greasy shed of my education, but by the intricacies of wrestling, and being told that I needed to prove that I had the bottle.

CHAPTER 3

The Round Ball

THERE WERE ONLY TWO of us who were amateur players in the Padgate Camp soccer team. The rest were professionals who played for their clubs on Saturdays and one of my fellow amateurs was a Scots international. Apart from Padgate, my credentials were Llanrwst Grammar and local league soccer when visiting home. I had also been invited to join Llanrwst Town who were in the high echelons of the Welsh League. I knew I could hold my own in this company, but there was a more pressing problem on the horizon. My weeks at camp were coming to an end. I knew that a world of sport, recreation and a cushy job in the health department would soon be replaced by a dole queue.

What to do? The £1 10/- RAF weekly wage at Padgate was not a fortune, but it was enough. Going home permanently presented a problem, since I was aware that most of my mates (who had not gone into farming) had left the village in search of work. I couldn't contemplate working regular hours, especially under a factory roof, and I had no skills worthy of mention, other than a handy left foot. I was not looking forward to the next few weeks. I remembered the advice given to my mother by one of our neighbours. "You should send him into the ministry," she said. No, not the ministry of defence, but the round collar ministry! But, for me, that was not an option.

It was Sergeant Brooking who asked me, "When you leave Taff, what are you going to do?"

"Dunno," I replied, and I must have looked a little downcast.

"Well how would you like to play football?"

It was a startling question, and I froze. "What do you mean, sir?" I asked.

"I'll have a word with Danny – we might be able to fix you up with something."

I could have said 'thank you' a thousand times. The following day I met Danny Marsh, the Padgate Camp captain, who was also a part-time player with Oldham Athletic.

"I thought you had been taken care of Taff – most of the other boys have been signed up," said Danny. "I'll be at Oldham training tomorrow night, and I'll have a word with George."

"George? George?" I said to myself. That could only mean George Hardwick, former captain of England, but now captain and manager of Oldham. Was this really happening? I told myself a hundred times not to count chickens, but over the next couple of days, as I awaited news from Danny, I became a nervous wreck. Danny was as good as his word. I was to meet *the* George Hardwick at the Oldham training ground on the Sunday morning. The three days seemed like an eternity to wait before meeting the man!

"How would you like a week's trial with Oldham young man? We'll see how you cope." He went on to say something else, but whatever it was, it was lost on me. A trial with Oldham Athletic of the Third Division North! It could have been the Third Division North Pole as far as I was concerned! This was it – it might only have been a trail offer, but that man could not have made me happier.

My first instinct was to write home and tell my mother the good news. Not that Mam would have known where Oldham was, but I was sure that she would pass on the news in the village. It was only a week's trial, and I knew that I had to make an impression, otherwise I would be shovelling silage for the rest of my life!

But there was unfinished business at Padgate – a last game for the camp against RAF Kirby. By this time I was playing with a level of confidence I had not enjoyed before. At the end of the game, which we won 1–0, a middle-aged gentleman approached me. "I gather you are the only unattached player in the team. How would you like a trial with Sunderland?" he asked. A few days earlier my future lay on the dole or something worse. Now I was being offered a chance to play at the mighty Sunderland. It was an amazing feeling and, after explaining that I had given my word to George Hardwick at Oldham, I thanked the man. It was all so unreal, and difficult to comprehend. What next? I didn't have to wait long for another shock.

On returning home, I realised quickly that my mother had not just told the village about the Oldham offer. She had told the whole world, or so it seemed. It was only a week's trial, but as far as Ysbyty Ifan was concerned, I had attained overnight cult status. On the Saturday I was due to play for Llanrwst against Rhyl in a Welsh League game, but my thoughts were on the playing fields of Oldham. That was until our chairman at Llanrwst, Will Jones, sidled up to me and in a quiet voice said, "Do you know, Orig, I think you have a good chance of being selected for the Wales amateur side against Scotland." My world was changing faster than I could run, or certainly think. Me – the Ted Drake of Ysbyty Ifan square – to wear the red shirt of Wales? Was it possible that all those penalty kicks taken against the village walls would now come to something? Could I possibly represent my country? If you had shown me a door, I would probably have flattened it!

The situation was clarified when a letter arrived from the Welsh FA confirming the invitation. A couple of lines also appeared in the *Daily Post*: "Orig Williams, former Llanrwst Grammar School football captain, who hails from the tiny upland village of Ysbyty Ifan, is booked for the final Welsh amateur trial, that is, if he does not sign professional forms for Oldham Athletic in the meantime."

Oh, calamity! Joy mixed with regret and many decisions to think through and make. To play for Wales in one game, but then, the thought of a potential career with Oldham? The prospect of playing for Wales at dominoes would have excited me. I wasn't sure if anyone from Ysbyty Ifan had ever represented Wales before. Sheepdog trials perhaps? Certainly we had National Eisteddfod winners in our midst. But I knew which one I had to pick. Oldham, the 'Letics' in the Third Division North, who were regularly watched by 20–30,000 crowds, was the choice. For once, my head had ruled my heart.

I watched the clock and the sun set during those last few days at RAF Padgate. How slowly time passes when your destiny awaits. I did nothing but fidget for my last remaining hours there. And so, off to Oldham, and a new nervousness. What if I failed to make the grade – what would they say at home? You turned down Wales? I could hear the chatter on the Ysbyty Ifan benches. "Had a trial with Oldham did our Orig. But didn't cut the mustard."

"Could have had a cap for Wales, he could."

"It would have been better for him to come home, and find some work here instead of gallivanting to England."

I arrived on the Sunday, and on Monday I trained with all the Oldham players. I knew that they had all seen it before – a young hopeful determined to make the grade in a week. A game was scheduled against Blackpool A – the very same club where Stanley Matthews, the king of wingers, displayed his skills on a weekly basis. His understudy, Sandy Brown, was to be my immediate opponent, and I knew that he was a very capable dribbling understudy to the great man.

The game went well: I closed him down and made sure that the ball wasn't wasted. And knowing full well that I was being scrutinised by my peers, I concentrated on every move. I knew that I was playing at a higher level than I'd ever achieved before. It was a promising start, and I enjoyed training with the senior players for a week. On the Saturday I was picked for the reserves against Rossendale. I could now at least add 'Oldham Athletic trial' to my name. That would count a lot in the Welsh League.

The game against Rossendale went well, and I had already settled in with a few of my new colleagues. We won 2–0, and since the senior team had also won their game there was a good feeling around the Oldham club that Saturday night.

Good feeling or not, however, I knew that I had a meeting with Mr Hardwick on the Sunday morning. What were my expectations? Probably a shake of the hands, a "thank you very much, thank you for coming", and a long journey home to the hills.

"The reserves did well yesterday Orig, didn't they," suggested Hardwick.

"Yes, sir, and your team as well, sir."

"Where do you think you are, Orig?" asked Hardwick. "You're

not in the RAF anymore, and I do not want to be called 'sir' when we play together, do you understand?"

"Understand what, ssi... Mr Hardwick?"

"The name is George, Orig, and what I am saying to you is that we are prepared to offer you a permanent contract. You'll get £10 for signing on, £10 a week during the season, and £7 a week during the summer weeks. Now then, do you accept?"

I am not sure what I said or how I replied, but I know I couldn't get my pen out quickly enough. I was now a professional footballer – being paid for what I loved to do – and it was five times the weekly wages of the boys on the farms. Accept? "Thank you... George", and to be honest, if given the authority, I would have knighted him there and then.

The dreams I had had of playing in front of large crowds in the football league were beginning to come true. The crowds in those days were huge, even for the Third Division. It was not unheard of to see crowds of 30–40,000... and I had the opportunity of playing with players who seemed to be constantly in the newspaper headlines. Oh, what ambitions I had! But, it didn't quite go according to plan. It all began well enough since I was 'adopted' on my first visit to the changing room. My mentor, guide and self-appointed instructor was to be Peter McKennan, a well-travelled and at one time an incredibly gifted footballer. He was a six-foot, brylcreemed-haired Scot who, by the time he had arrived at Oldham, via Patrick Thistle, West Brom, West Ham and Middlesborough, had clearly been worn down by injuries, which included a fragile ankle.

Though he had received little schooling, he was known as McKennan MA BA or MA BA McKennan. These were names given to him because, due to his lack of mobility, he insisted that every pass should arrive at his feet, so that he could direct matters from a square yard. MA BA stood for 'My Ball' and as such, you obeyed. The language from McKennan, if his instructions were ignored, was vicious and threatening.

At one stage in his career, he could dribble away, beating man after man, and should have been capped by his country, but, as befitting a D-Day landing station commander, he was no quitter, and woe betide anyone who crossed him. But he had been ravaged by injuries and the spark was no longer there – but nobody dared to tell him that. And he was *my* mentor.

"You'll do all the training laps with me, and at my pace. Do you understand chuchter?" Naturally, I had no idea what a 'chuchter' was, but when I later gathered it was an uncomplimentary term for a highland bumpkin, it was, I suppose, a fairly accurate assessment of a green-behind-the-ears youngster from Ysbyty Ifan!

What I wasn't prepared for was McKennan's extra-curricular activities. He was a man with a vile temper and was used to having his way. This became patently obvious one night as he tried to pass a double-decker bus on our way to the dog racing at White City in Manchester. The bus driver would not yield to McKennan in his flashy sports car. So, shouting obscenities as he stopped at traffic lights, he pulled the poor man from his seat and banged his head into one of the bus headlights. This is a dangerous man I thought – but as he had enlisted me as his dog racing companion for my duration at Oldham, there was little I could do. He was convinced that I brought him luck. I must have to a certain extent, because he had no idea about the form of the dogs – yet he was successful with several winners.

As a young fringe player, I knew that I wouldn't be at Oldham for very long unless I made an impression. But what transpired was not the impression I had intended. We were on our way to play Rochdale reserves, who had recently signed Eric Betts from West Ham for a handsome £6,000 fee. He was a very talented left-winger. He'd been selected to play against us – in order that the Rochdale management could take a look at his playing abilities. George Hardwick decided to give me the responsibility of looking after him – from the right half position. Now, everybody knew that I was a left footer, so this new position was not to my liking at all. And so it proved, as Betts quickly exposed my discomfort, making me look a real prat. I knew that I had to do something to slow him down, and when he attempted for the umpteenth time to go around me, I deliberately floored him. It took him some time to recover, since he was probably able to count 6,000 stars.

"Penalty," shouted the Rochdale players, and the referee had no hesitation. We lost the game by that single goal.

There was an angry mood on the homeward bus, and most of that anger was directed towards me. After all, the boys had lost their bonus. On that bus was one Alan Ball senior, the father of Alan Ball, England's 1966 World Cup winning hero. When the reserves' manager Herbert Gartside told me quietly that I should not have given the penalty away, Ball senior heard him and in a not so quiet a voice said, "Quite agree Mr Gartside... no need for it at all... totally unnecessary." Bloody bootlicker! So when Mr Ball went to fetch his kit bag at the back of the bus, I followed him and told him to mind his business. He smiled at me. That was it! I decked him as well, and I knew my Oldham days were spent. It took only a few minutes to realise that I had blown it. I wouldn't be playing in front of 40,000 crowds at Oldham, or even playing for Wales now.

Mr Hardwick called me in. He was in sombre mood, and quickly told me that Shrewsbury Town were looking for a left half. At least it was an offer, since prolonging my stay at Boundary Park was not an option. I packed my bags and left for Gay Meadow.

Shrewsbury was something of a culture shock. Oldham was a fanatical football town, a busy industrial town and a buoyant place. Shrewsbury was an historical town, full of beautiful buildings. The football club had a small compact ground – and sounded like a convent compared with the 'Latics' chorus. It was also short of characters like MA BA McKenna. But it was a lifeline and a chance to redeem myself.

Some two months passed at Shrewsbury and I must have made a favourably impression, since the manager hinted that a good game for the reserves on Saturday would see me making a debut for the club on the following weekend. Our match was against Burton Albion, fellow contenders for the top of the table slot in the Midland League. It was going to be highly competitive.

In fact, it was an enjoyable game, and I knew that I was handling everything well. We were on level pegging when their left wing broke through to pose a threat. I had my man marked. Then the winger let go with a hard low cross, about four feet off the ground. I had a split second decision to make – kick or head away. The ball hit me on the head and I was out cold – and came to my senses, or part of them, in Burton-on-Trent Memorial Hospital three days later.

Absolute calamity! The dismissal from Oldham was my doing. But this was a cruel blow – I was told that I had a blood clot and that it was so near the brain that any movement might paralyse me for life. I was rested and motionless on a bed of wooden planks, strapped in by leather belts for three weeks, with only one thought in mind – would I ever play football again?

It was total frustration. Countless hours of viewing the same windowpane and listening to the nurses chatter near the kettle. But would they talk to me about what I wanted to talk about. No fear! I was left to talk to my imagination, and that wasn't responding either! After three excruciatingly long weeks, the matron entered and announced that I was going to be released the next day, but only after I had spoken to the doctor. The mere mention of home was enough to create a rush of blood. I could convalesce on the village bench and spend days stretching yarns that were fully stretched already. I could go hunting, or spend some time with my friend Huw Sel the carpenter. I could do anything I wanted to do. "But on no account can your ever play football again," said the doctor. "If you do, it could either kill you, or paralyse you for life." I pleaded with him and told him there was nothing else I could do. I didn't have qualifications, just a left leg and a dodgy head. I begged him to reconsider. He could see that I was clutching for some kind of hope, and he relented, asking me to come back – in a year's time! At least it was something. Not much, I grant you.

Ysbyty Ifan had not changed. They were still repeating the same old stories, but wanted to know about England. Mothers muttered about football being a waste of time, and that I should get a proper job. The young lads had gone, never to return. I couldn't sit on a bench for twelve months, and so Huw decided to take me on as his carpentry apprentice. So now I had a good left leg, a dodgy head and two left hands! There was no future for me in the timber industry.

Time went by very slowly. Huw did invite me to a Welsh nationalist rally at Beddgelert where the party's leader Gwynfor Evans inspired both of us with a 'call to action' speech. I didn't need much persuading in that direction, neither did Huw, for that matter, since our village had been a hot-bed of nationalistic fervour for centuries. True, there were strangers in our midst with strange political ideas and foreign ideas. We knew who they were, too. If they didn't speak to you when passing in the street, you knew they were strangers or 'invaders'. We had been taught to be on our guard since the war.

But one day, a stranger did come to see me. At least, that is, he wasn't from Ysbyty Ifan, but I did know who he was. He was a huge hero of mine! It was Tommy Jones of Everton and Wales – I couldn't believe it. I had followed his career in the newspapers and I could recall his games for Wales, especially when we had beaten the Scots by three goals to one. Tommy ranked alongside John Charles, Ivor Allchurch and Ryan Giggs as Welsh greats. Tommy Jones of Everton was in Ysbyty Ifan – and had come to see me! He had shocked everyone by leaving Everton to become manager of Pwllheli in the Welsh League. He was still only thirty-one years old and had at least five years of top-flight football before him. But he had wanted to return home. What was even more astonishing was that he invited me to play for Pwllheli. Alas, I had to tell him about my medical condition, and that, technically, I was still on Shrewsbury's books. However, he had already spoken to Shrewsbury and they were happy to release me from my contract. It was up to me and whether I wanted to have a medical check-up. No sooner had he gone, I arranged for a medical at Burton-on-Trent Hospital.

I am still not sure whether my medical examiner was looking for evidence of a blood clot or whether he was trying to establish whether I had a brain. It took an eternity, and though I knew there wasn't much of anything there, he eventually gave up. "Your condition is clear, Mr Williams," meaning that there was nothing there. "Does that mean I can play football, Doc?" I asked.

"I think it does, but do take care."

It is astonishing how emotions fluctuate. I had shuffled into the hospital fearing the worst, and I nearly jumped through a window to get out of there. There was no holding me back now – but what to do? I had a choice between Shrewsbury Town (who had incidentally replaced me) and Pwllheli, a seaside town on the Llŷn peninsular. I had no great affinity with Shrewsbury, and didn't particularly like the place. But Pwllheli was smaller, and although Tommy Jones had tried to persuade me that the Welsh League would be easier than the Third Division of the Football League, I didn't believe a word of it. There were more 'nutters' in the Welsh League, and certainly more local football derbies.

Tommy invited me to Pwllheli, since he knew I had some lingering doubts about joining his club. But these feelings did not last long. I did feel a little out of it being a 'Williams' though.

The Pwllheli owners were Dr Jones and Mr T M Jones, a visionary pair who had invited Mr T G Jones to become their manager. Tommy, in turn, had become the owner of the largest hotel in the town, the Tower. Pwllheli, much to my delight, was predominantly a Welsh-speaking town and naturally the Tower had been translated to Y Tŵr, and hence Tommy Jones was known locally as 'Tom Tŵr'. He had been quickly embraced by the community, and as he was a star with Everton and Wales, he was known as the prince of the region.

Tommy enthused about his ambition for the Pwllheli club. Not only that, he also managed to fix me up with a part-time job at the nearby holiday camp and find me first-class lodgings. I would play alongside him in the team defence. Shrewsbury had already become a distant memory.

I was not the only new recruit. The Pwllheli team was a mixture of local- and Liverpool-based players, and Tommy had begun moulding a team, which he wanted to play in a particular way. He was, as you'd expect, immensely knowledgeable about patterns of play and about how to adjust to situations and opponents. He wouldn't entertain slouches or those who would not listen. He had no respect for authority, either, especially the Football Association of Wales, even though he had represented his country on several occasions. I remember one FAW official entering the Pwllheli dressing room at half-time when Tommy was having a rant. The bigwig had scarcely opened his mouth before Tommy had told him to 'piss off'.

I heard on the grapevine that we had signed a new player from Nefyn, a small coastal village, now better known as the home of the singer Duffy. The player's name was Idris Wyn, and he played at right back. He was to become a close personal friend of mine for life. There was very little sophistication about him. If Tommy had asked him to run through a brick wall, Idris would have obliged. He was totally fearless. Tommy's plan was – as he controlled matters as captain, manager and centre-half – to make us the most feared defence in the league. The local fans took to Idris immediately, with one of the crowd crowning him as 'Tarw Nefyn' – the Nefyn Bull. The name stuck, and from that time generations have never known his real name.

He was a full-time plasterer. By that I mean he applied his trade techniques to opposition players on the football pitch as well. I would grimace if a player attempted to get the better of him, since I knew the eventual outcome. He roamed our half of the field in search of intruders, with Tommy urging me on to do likewise. There were to be no prisoners, and certainly no trespassers. The job had not been done until the opposition had fear in their eyes.

There was one incident which illustrates Tarw Nefyn's determination and lack of fear. We had managed to get through the early rounds of the Welsh Cup. Our next opposition was Swansea Town, as they were known then. Swansea had a marvellous crop of talented youngsters, including the Allchurch brothers, Mel Charles, Terry Medwin and one Cliff Jones. The latter had been an absolute thorn on the playing field, as his pace was astonishing and we had difficulty containing his darting runs. Then, suddenly, Jones broke through again, and Tarw set out at full-pace to nail his man. Both were set for a mighty collision, when Cliff Jones suddenly produced an extra gear. Tarw, unfortunately, had already launched himself. He missed his man, but cleared the Vetch Field perimeter wall and ended up in the crowd. He was not amused, especially when we asked him where he had been!

Under Tommy's tutelage we became a feared pair, and became the butt of abuse wherever we played. But there was more to Tommy's coaching than running around as his henchmen. He taught us how to tackle, retain and distribute. The man knew his stuff, and we were more than willing pupils. Tommy could read the game, and we were his two bookends.

He was not short of a sharp word either. "Orig," he once told me, "if that winger walks off the field at the end of this game, you are a bloody coward." With a razor-sharp tongue, it was little wonder (despite moulding a formidable outfit like Pwllheli) that Tommy did not court favour with the powers of the game in Wales. Few could anyway, since there were more committee men than players. This was the body that once left a player behind so that a committee man could have a seat on a plane on an away trip.

Scotland and England had appointed full-time national managers. The Welsh FA, like Snowdonia's sheep, followed suit. Two men were invited to apply and be interviewed by those who 'knew' the game, or thought they did. One applicant was Dave Bowen, formerly from Arsenal but then manager of Northampton Town. The other one was Tommy, who had to be persuaded to become involved. Both were excellent candidates, but were hardly, in football terms, meeting their peers at the interview. In football matters the Welsh FA had always posed as paupers. Tommy did not get the job.

But he did move on – and so did we. Tommy became manager of Bangor City – and with distinction too. They won the Welsh Cup, and in so doing qualified for the European Cup. The home fixture in Bangor, against Italian champions FC Napoli was won, but the away game lost. The play-off was held at Highbury in London, Bangor lost 2–1 in a replay. It was a season to remember for Tommy – a side of amateurs and part-timers giving the pride of Italy a run for their money. Tarw decided to switch clubs and moved to Caernarfon, and I ventured south to play in the South Wales League for Aberystwyth.

I suppose, in a way, Tommy had taught us not to respect the opposition. They were there to be intimidated. This philosophy – if you could call it that – was extended as well to anyone in authority, and that included the Football Association of Wales. These were well-matured committee men, but few had played the game at any respectable level. Whatever they seemed to do, whatever edicts they passed down were met with vociferous opposition by the grass-roots. It was inevitable that I would collide with them. They enjoyed their foreign trips – fifteen players and ten committee men, first-class journeys to South America with all expenses paid – and quite unable to realise that investment was required within the game.

I didn't stay long at Aberystwyth, since the travelling to the opposing south Wales clubs every other weekend, on the meandering roads of Wales, was too tiring. I signed for Penmaenmawr, linking up with Tarw Nefyn once again. Then came an invitation to become the player-manager of my old club Pwllheli.

This was indeed a challenge, since I knew that filling the position once occupied by Tommy Jones of Everton and Wales would attract comparisons and possible resentment. But, by now, I was seasoned enough to know that trawling the fields of Cheshire and Deeside for good players was not a productive scouting policy. True, there were gifted players, but they played for the money and not with their hearts. Far better, in my opinion, was the discovery of less-gifted local players who had pride and a little attitude. And that last attribute I had in abundance – and it would constantly get me in trouble.

The Pwllheli club produced a match programme, and inevitably, at that level of the game, it had very little content. So I started writing a manager's column. Naturally, I chose to attack the FAW on a weekly basis, accusing them of not knowing anything about the game, of being more concerned with their benefits rather than anyone's future or welfare. The referees they appointed – apart from a few exceptions – came in for some stick as well. It went down well with the locals, who were initially surprised that I could write at all!

However, news of the column reached the powers at the Football Association. The Pwllheli Club was reprimanded and I was not to continue writing the column under any circumstances. I was also banned from playing for a week for 'bringing the game to disrepute'. I have no doubt that within the folders and drawers of the Welsh FA, a file had been opened marked Orig Williams. It became a well-thumbed, exceptionally thick folder by the time I had finished with the game. I told anyone who would listen to me what the FA stood for in terms of its contribution to Welsh football.

I had a successful time at Pwllheli. We reached the North Wales Challenge Cup Final against Blaenau Ffestiniog – a game that was played at Farrar Road, Bangor. The Cup Final was held out of season, but that also meant that players at other clubs were also 'out of contract'. So I borrowed or 'contracted' two good players from Ellesmere Port for the Bangor game. We won! And then, all hell broke loose! The FAW eventually changed its own rules – and my personal file became even thicker.

During this time it became apparent that our attendances were not what they should be. The issue of supporters was a concern, since the income from them was our only means of survival. We couldn't appeal for support from the FAW, since we knew what we would get. FA again. Other managers were complaining too, and gradually the reason behind the falling gate dawned on us.

ITV had started to show professional wrestling at 4 o'clock on Saturday afternoons. It had become an overnight success and the choice of being entertained in the warmth of your home as opposed to being out in the cold, rain-swept football grounds, was a non-starter. We simply could not compete. It wasn't expensive to watch us – a few bob, but sitting at home with a can of beer and watching flying bodies, holds and submissions was a far better proposition. If we had received some financial help to improve our grounds and spectator facilities in those days, it might have helped. But that would have taken vision from the game's governors. The game in Wales yet again received nothing.

But our cup in some ways was overflowing at Pwllheli. We reached the fifth round of the Welsh Cup. The game was away against Oswestry, and we comfortably won by six goals to nil. If you believe in fate, then ironically it was the visit to an Oswestry fish and chip shop after the game which was to have a marked effect on my life. I was famished, but at the same time transfixed by a poster on the chippie wall, promoting a night of wrestling in Oswestry on the following Saturday. The promoter was Tommy Newton, the man who had taught me the rudiments at his sweaty Manchester shed a few years back. I had to be there, no matter what.

Fortunately, our game the following week was at Colwyn Bay, so driving to Oswestry after the match was not a problem. The main bout was advertised as being between Doctor Death, the horrific masked executioner, and gypsy Joe Savoldi, the all-action Romany Grappler. I couldn't wait. As soon as our game had finished in Colwyn Bay, I headed towards the venue in Oswestry. I arrived in good time, but was astonished to see a long queue of about five hundred people waiting to get in. These people were either paying ten shillings for a seat, or five shillings for a standing place. The queue was also getting longer. Pwllheli would be lucky to get a 300 crowd paying three shillings for the stand and two shillings for a field entrance.

I eventually got inside to see that the wrestling bouts had already started. It was packed out with 1,000 people inside. These were men, women and a fair number of children who had come to be entertained. It was dramatically dark, and the ring was highlighted by bright lights through the smoke-filled arena. Tommy Newton, my friend, was the referee and, of course, promoter.

Eventually Doctor Death arrived. The place went berserk, with everyone shouting abuse at the masked villain, whilst applauding Joe as the hero. The crowd were on their feet, waving their arms, pointing menacingly towards Doctor Death. The place was ablaze with emotion, and the two wrestlers were master manipulators of the situation. Joe was soon forced to retire, due to the fact that one of his eyes had started to bleed profusely. The crowd were on their seats and threatening to throw a few seats at the masked man. The language was something else, especially from the women! It was tremendous stuff and great drama. Thoroughly impressed, I went looking for my old friend Tommy Newton.

I knocked on his door and was immediately made welcome. "Good God! Orig? What are you doing here? Do you know, I have been thinking about you, but didn't know where you were, or how to get hold of you. Come in!" It was the same old Tommy – full of enthusiasm. "Did you see the wrestling? Did you see and hear that reaction?" I told him that I had enjoyed myself, especially the reaction of the large crowd. Then he shocked me. "Well, how do you fancy being a wrestler Orig? You sort of know the moves, and I could train you up. What do you think?"

I didn't think – I was dumbfounded. He explained that wrestling was now big business, due to the television coverage, with every promoter struggling to find wrestlers, with some even having to go on recruiting drives in pubs and dances where it was known that fights would often break out. "You could do it, Orig. I have no doubt about that," he said. "You are fit, large and strong – ideal material." I explained to Tommy about my ties with football and I could see his disappointment. However, he had planted a new idea in my head. It was something that I could do when the legs couldn't carry me through the muddy fields of north Wales any more. We left on good terms, and I promised to be in touch. I wasn't *quite* finished with the round ball. My next phase was to be the most colourful yet.

One of the fundamental problems with football in north Wales was the lack of regulations governing transfers of players from outside the area. Every Saturday, cars, full of footballers, would arrive in various towns and villages: from Chester, Liverpool and even Manchester. Every manager wanted to win games, so the inevitable easy route was to hire outside talent. I admit that I was guilty of this, but that still didn't make it right. These players, good as they were, had no loyalty except to the match-fee and the travelling expenses. The end result was that local players hardly had an opportunity to develop their skills, other than in the local county leagues.

At the end of the season, these mercenaries would look around for the best deal offered, since they were not contractually bound to any club. So, in five years, one player or even a car full of players could have played for five different clubs. The system was at fault, and the system was the responsibility of my FA friends! An invitation to become player-manager of Nantlle Vale gave me the opportunity to put a stop to all of this. The Nantlle Vale committee had extended the invitation and had insisted that they would prefer a team of local lads as Nantlle was an exceptionally strong Welsh-speaking area. So, next, I was on my way to Nantlle Vale.

CHAPTER 4

Nantlle Vale

The Dirtiest Team in the League

CALL ME PAROCHIAL, INSULAR, stubborn and fiercely Welsh – and I will proudly plead guilty to all charges, in my native tongue. It is the way of the world to protect your own, and my world was based in a hotbed of Welsh nationalism. There is no greater sin in my book than not being proud of one's own acre, and of one's own people.

I have had many fierce discussions with far more learned people than I, but my belief is that you cannot feel truly Welsh unless you speak the language. How can you know of your heritage unless you understand the language of bards, prophets, warriors and heroes? There have been magnificent people who have represented Wales and its affairs without being able to speak the language. And it is to their immense credit that they have done so within their limitations. But I cannot accept that their blood is as red as mine.

Perhaps I was born a few centuries too late, since I would have eagerly enlisted in Glyndŵr's armies in driving the Norman and English landlords from our land. I am also a born romanticist, as my wife Wendy will vouch for, and there is nothing I like more than reciting the defiant words of the Welsh poets, Cynan, T H Parry-Williams or Gwenallt when alone or driving the car. So, my views on being Welsh could start a few more arguments! So with that background, I set about life – inspired by defiance rather than diplomacy, stubbornness rather than sensitivity, with more brawn than brain – and ready for battle. I did not have to wait long for action.

For a number of years, I had been aware of what was happening on north Wales's football pitches, unlike the committee men of the Welsh FA. As already mentioned, every weekend would see cars, filled with soccer players from Liverpool, Chester and Manchester, destined for towns and villages that they could not even pronounce. These were football mercenaries who would play for a team for a season and then play for another the next season.

And, yes, I too became guilty of being involved in recruiting some of these mercenaries. As a manager you wanted the best team, and unfortunately I too went to distant parts to recruit a few players. Players could move from one club to another at the end of the season – the end result was a football cattle market. There were no high transfer fees, just match fees, and any additional bonus system was done under the counter. It could have been halted, since there were enough Welsh FA committee men based in north Wales to form two teams, but alas – FA inaction once again. It was all so wrong!

Then, I received the phone call inviting me to become player-manager of Nantlle Vale – a club located in the heartland of nationalistic Wales. It was close to Snowdon, and therefore closer to heaven than most clubs, and it certainly had no ambitions of recruiting mercenaries. They could not afford much in monetary terms. In fact, my weekly budget to cater for all players was to be the princely sum of £15. I wonder how Alex Ferguson would have reacted to that! Fifteen quid a week to run the whole club – expenses, training, transport – the bloody lot! But, I could not have been happier! Given free reign I knew what I had to do, and my first call was to my trusted friend – Tarw Nefyn. I explained to him that we would be a local Welsh side and we didn't want any weekend foreigners. The language would be Welsh and we would not yield to anyone. With Tarw on board, others came to arms and responded to the call. To be invited was almost like being given a Welsh cap!

The club already had Robin Ken on its books – he had recently returned home after a spell with Wrexham. He was a strong non-yielding type – a mountain man and a half-back. With Tarw in the centre, flanked by me and Robin, I knew that only a Snowdon volcanic eruption would unsettle us. Gifted players score goals, but defences win leagues, and I was sure that few teams would relish the prospect of facing us three.

Gradually the team came together – from Ffestiniog, Bethesda and Caernarfon. They were all Welsh speaking, mainly local lads, hard as nails – with a point to prove. You didn't need newspapers to tell the locals what we were planning. Word got around that Orig Williams was forming a mountain guerrilla soccer team at Nantlle Vale – a team full of Norman Hunter types. I did not object to the advanced publicity. It would make us feared, and we would become known as 'the dirtiest team in the league'. Dirty? No, just hard.

Rarely did I have to ask for effort, but if I did, it was always the same call to arms. We played for Wales and for the flag. Thankfully there was someone always on hand to open the changing room door before letting my troops out to battle!

The opposing teams would have their full quota of imported English players, full of white-collar administrators, teachers and bankers. My boys were raw sons of the mountains, and we could not wait to get stuck in. And there I was, with a weekly managerial budget of £15. But these boys did not play for pay; they were playing for themselves, Nantlle Vale and Wales! Take me seriously when I say I would not have liked to play against us.

If an opponent tried to get the upper hand, he'd be introduced to a Nantlle shoulder charge, and some of them would have moved bulls. If the opposition injured one of our players, he would learn how uncomfortable the beds were in the local hospital. We followed the edict of that great Welshman and British Lions coach Carwyn James, and we got our retaliation in first. I always maintained that we were not a dirty team, but hard. Others took a different view, especially the referees.

Word got around about the 'henchmen' or the 'Nantlle commandos' and worse. In the unlikely event that we would have retained our full complement of players by the end of the game, with yours truly being offered 'an early bath' more often than the rest, we would make sure that at least we were playing against the same number of players. If we were one down, then measures had to be taken to balance the numbers.

I had no problem generating motivation. It was always the 'us' against 'them' approach. A few words of patriotic encouragement at half-time would always produce results – and a few incidents. Alas, whereas our playing approach attracted all manner of condemnation from opposition clubs, so too did our linguistic policy, as we would all naturally speak Welsh to each other. Visiting referees were rarely Welsh speaking, and suspected that they were the subject of our, and indeed the local support's banter. There was an element of truth in the accusation, since we were all aware of the referee's positioning. Maybe more than a little mischief was conducted when the referee had his back turned, but I do believe that we were penalised against for trivial incidents as their retaliation. Little wonder that Nantlle's exploits attracted more press and headlines than the rest of the league combined. The local reporters knew that a visit to a Nantlle game would rarely fail to provide a headline.

However, the committee men of the game dealt us a severe blow. Overnight, a law change caused us much consternation and prompted us to call a summit meeting. No longer were attacking players allowed to touch, barge or have any physical contact with opposing goalkeepers. What was the game coming to? Just imagine telling Trevor Ford that his weaponry had been taken away from him? The intimidation of the goalie was a Nantlle tour de force! We all felt neutered and thought that this was an extreme measure, which called for an extreme response.

Our next game was at Prestatyn, and we knew that the opposition goalie was a six-foot colossus – but his size was not matched by his courage. The changing rooms at Prestatyn, like in so many clubs, were housed in a Portakabin, with thin dividing walls between home and visiting dressing rooms. Tarw and I hatched a plan. A few minutes before kick-off, Tarw and I conducted a very loud team talk, whilst leaning against the dividing wall. "Ignore the new law," I told him, "just plant one on him as soon as you can." Tarw, who, under the old law was a much-feared visitor in the opposition penalty box, needed little encouragement. "Just make sure, he knows you are there." "Don't worry," he replied, "I'll put him in the local cemetery." We knew that the opposing goalie would be listening. For the first ten minutes of the game, the opposition goalkeeper watched us like a fidgeting squirrel, but he was also having a blinder. And that was not on! "OK Tarw, this is what we will do. Next corner, you go in front of him, I will go behind. At least one of us will have a shot at him." Across came the ball, and down went the goalie, screaming in pain. We were collectively rebuked by the referee because, though he suspected foul play, he could not identify the culprit. But the goalie could – he thought we were all to blame, and promptly decided to walk off the field. We had demolished his confidence. There were weekly incidents, and I knew we were walking a tight rope. Sooner, rather than later, we would be called to answer and account for our behaviour.

It was known in the village that I had a hankering for the wrestling game, and when the referee, a Mr McManus from Chester, arrived at Connah's Quay for our game there, it inspired all manner of comment. Mick McManus was already a Saturday afternoon wrestling favourite on the box. Our Mr McManus was certainly not built for any ring. He was short and, as is so often the case, was efficiently fussy with his whistle. The support on the touchline didn't help either. "McManus will have you Orig!" they shouted, or "Watch out McManus – Williams will give you one." The referee heard everything, and the more nervous he got, the more intolerable he became.

Then it happened. The match, already a fractious affair, turned into a big bust up and I was singled out, quite correctly, as the guilty assailant. In stepped the little one with the whistle and, by this time, I had really taken a dislike to him. He called me over, but I stood my ground. I was not going to be lectured by this pipsqueak. "Off," he shouted, pointing towards the dressing room. "Off you go!" as the pitch of his voice reached screaming point. He pointed his finger again and this time it was too much for me. I bit his finger, and held on tight!

The screams could be heard all over Connah's Quay. "You are a lunatic. Let go! Let go!" But I wouldn't, and I dragged him all the way to the dressing-room door before releasing McManus and his finger. The headlines were predictable: 'McManus sees Williams off.' I knew I was going to be disciplined. I was no stranger to Football Association of Wales disciplinary hearings, but this one was being held in Old Colwyn and chaired by the Association's Mr Herbert Powell. Mr McManus was also there, in a suit, bespectacled and looking every part the seasoned Old Bailey barrister. He produced his evidence – if the man could not referee, he could certainly prepare a case. He claimed that the 'bite' had resulted in a hospital anti-tetanus injection and he was still having pains that kept him awake at night.

His eloquence and reasoned approach was obviously carrying the day. Then, it was my turn.

I questioned the validity of the anti-tetanus treatment, by pulling out my false teeth, making sure that the disciplinary bench realised that they were plastic! I was banned for three weeks.

Mud sticks and so does a bad reputation. We didn't question our approach to the game. We couldn't, because it was the only one we knew. We couldn't compete with the imported dribblers from over the border, so the siege mentality remained unchanged. Nor were we fashionable. One walk through Pen-y-groes or Bethesda would ascertain that this was not a fashionable area. But we had a common bond of defiance that few could challenge, let alone defeat. But this was to come to an end, ironically at the beginning of the next season. It was inevitable, and it was more predictable that we would face disciplinary action again.

The game was in Llandudno and they were a team who were graced with imported, paid soccer evacuees and captained by Scotsman John Curry. The referee was a stranger – which I took to be a good omen, since he might not have been aware of any previous misdemeanours on our part. Tarw and I went into our usual banter of trying to undermine the opposition. "Do you want to see your wife tonight, mate? Or would you like to visit the C and A infirmary in Bangor?"

"Hey you, any more fairies like you at home?"

"See that man over there? He plays football on Saturdays. Otherwise he's a week-day psychopath."

"All Englishmen are cowards."

This went on for a while, and it had the desired effect. Unfortunately, the referee had been listening as well, and he blew his whistle. He was pretty ashen faced. "Cut all this chatter out. I've never heard anything like it and won't tolerate it, do you understand?" The game went on for a while, and then I put in a fair, but hard tackle. Down went my opponent, screaming his head off and, although it wasn't a dirty tackle, I was given my usual marching orders. But, before leaving, I told Tarw to control the boys, as I did sincerely think we were capable of beating this lot.

I hadn't finished untying my boot laces in the changing room when the door opened and Robin Ken, my right-back entered. He, too, had been sent off for striking John Curry, the opposing captain. And it wasn't long before the door opened again, with Tarw entering this time. "What the hell is going on?" I asked.

"Two more sent off," he replied, "me, and one of them, and that little p*** has abandoned the game!" Curtains – I could see curtains! I could also see headlines as well, and I was not to be disappointed.

The letter of summons to another disciplinary hearing was also predictable. This hearing was to be held in Rhyl Town Hall, with a seating capacity of up to five hundred people. But for this hearing there were only eight of us. We outnumbered the FA committee and the referee. I was there, accompanied by Tarw, Robin Ken and the opposing captain John Curry – who ironically was a friend of mine.

The chairman of this FAW meeting was Herbert Powell once again – a man more renowned for his administrative eloquence rather than any football skill. The referee was also in attendance and he had written a thesis on the whole affair. How was it that these referees could write with such authority and phraseology, but couldn't control a game to save their lives? White-collar boys, no doubt. The referee's evidence was read out by Mr Powell, who paused at every damning phrase. By the time he finished, I reckoned they were building a guillotine on the Rhyl promenade, such was the severity of the report's accusations. We were characterised as 'Welsh mountain goats' – and that was one of the more complimentary remarks.

John Curry also gave his evidence. Nothing wrong with that, I thought. It was sincere, as he reported the facts without any side remarks. The accused were next. We were not allowed any kind of counsel and the evidence was to be given in English – the days of a Welshman being able to present his evidence in his own language was years in the future.

"On behalf of my learned 'mountain goats'," I began, having watched a few Perry Mason courtroom dramas, "I would like to ask the referee some questions." This little pen pusher from Chester was not going to be given a free ride.

"Sir," I said, addressing the once ashen-faced official, but who was now transparent with arteries and corpuscles showing. "Had you heard of Nantlle Vale, before you came to officiate us?"

"Yes, I had," he replied.

"And had you heard of our reputation? Were we a good team? A combative team? Or a dirty team?"

"A dirty team, by all accounts," he answered.

"So," I said, going for the jugular, "You were not looking forward to the game?"

"No, I wasn't," he replied. I dismissed him there and then and before he had a chance of elaborating, I turned to the chairman Herbert Powell. "Esteemed Sir. As you will have witnessed, this man, the referee, was clearly prejudiced before he arrived to officiate. He was, for whatever reason, frightened and extremely nervous of the game he was about to officiate. He was, in my humble opinion, the wrong man to have been asked to referee this game."

This was our defence. I sat down, and the FA retired to consider their verdict.

Tarw, sitting alongside understood little of what was said, and Robin was not that much wiser. The jury took half an hour to reach their verdict. They returned, sombre and pensive, with Mr

Powell looking particularly thoughtful. It was the beginning of the season, and if we were to be severely punished, Nantlle Vale was doomed to obscurity – a place where I am sure the Welsh FA would have gladly paid the fare. I looked at them and I knew that not one of them had played a game of competitive football in their lives. Mr Powell cleared his throat, and shuffled his papers. "Mr Williams, this is not the first time we have met. In fact, throughout the records of the Football Association of Wales, you are the one individual who has been sent off from the field of play more than anyone in our history. You have continually brought the game into disrepute." (I could hear them testing the gallows on the promenade.) "You are clearly a man who is anti-establishment, and you have no regard for the game. You have the worst disciplinary record in the league."

"Thank you, sir." I replied. That did not go down well.

"We have," he continued, "given serious consideration of imposing a *sine die* suspension in your case." (I knew I would have to explain that one to Tarw later). "But in lieu of your compassionate and well-reasoned statements here today, we have decided to impose a lesser ban of twenty-four weeks upon you. I might add that you should consider pursuing a career in law, since you appear to have a gift for that. However, Mr Williams, in case you have any doubt, should you ever appear before an FAW disciplinary committee again, for whatever reason, you will be banned *sine die*. Do I make myself understood?" Tarw and Robin were each banned for two weeks, and we all retired, with John Curry in tow, to celebrate at the nearby Mona Hotel. I explained to Tarw what *sine die* meant, and we celebrated hard and heartedly for the whole day!

Yet, in a reflective moment, I knew the game was up. The way Nantlle played the game, it was inevitable that a return visit to the disciplinary panel was on the cards. I couldn't tell my warriors to play a different game since they would not have understood – as they enjoyed living 'on the edge'. Mr Powell's words stayed with me for a few days. If I returned to face him, I'd have no future as far as my football career was concerned. It was time to move on and place my size ten boots in a box.

I phoned Tommy Newton, my old wrestling tutor in Manchester. "Time to give football a rest," was his advice. He invited me down to the sweat parlour he called a gym for a training week or 'refresher course', and then invited me to join his gang on the road in Ireland. "The world is your oyster," he said, and I was prepared to believe him.

I received what politely could be called a rudimentary crash course in wrestling. The first lesson was to fall properly without causing too much damage. The next lessons were devoted to the Japanese Stranglehold, Indian Death-lock, Full Nelson, Irish Whip and the Bear Hug – it was going to be a long education.

"You're made for this game," he told me. "You're strong, you have the right build and I think you'll put up with anything, and that last factor is essential for a wrestler." Little did I know that the last clause of that sentence was to be severely tested in various parts of the world.

I returned from Ireland and spent a few months touring north-east Lancashire and Scotland. It was a hugely instructive time, not only in the ring, but also adapting to the lifestyle of the wrestlers. There were few comforts. You travelled, put up the ring, sold the tickets, entertained the punters and slept rough. Wherever we went I would try to get home to see the boys at Nantlle, all of them eagerly awaiting news of my new profession. It wasn't quite the same anymore, and though the banter would remain for years after receiving my *sine die* warning, I knew that a professional wrestling career could match my academic achievements – none!

"You've got to learn the game from scratch," said Tommy. "So I am going to send you down to Cornwall to a good friend of mine, Mickey Kiely. He runs the shows in all the fairs. He'll teach you all you need to know."

CHAPTER 5

In the beginning, there was Bodmin

PEOPLE WHO BEGIN THEIR careers on the bottom rung before rising to the top are much revered. Whatever their line of work, they are able to progress and relate their practical experiences to new-found challenges and challengers.

So there I was, sent or sentenced, beginning my wrestling apprenticeship in the bowels of Penzance, Redruth and Bodmin – likeable Cornish towns by day, but by night, transformed by our wrestling fairs into a melee of drunken brawling fairground revelling. This was to be my 'schooling' to progress as a fledgling wrestler.

My tutor, Mickey Kiely, was an impressive showman with action and words. It was his wrestling booth, his show, his tour, and we were sandwiched on the field between the Wall of Death and the stripping ladies. We were always allocated the same position at each fair. The roar of the Wall of Death motorbikes would summon the single men. The stripper ladies would pull others in with their crude calls, "Come in here, luv, and see some real tits!" And Mickey Kiely would challenge pundits by shouting, "Come in here, boy, and show her you're a man". It was a tried and tested marketing formula, which somehow worked. The smell, or rather stench and the noise of the booth would stay with me forever. It stank of embrocation, sweat, resin and leather. We would put the tent and booth up and then take it down, we slept rough – and all for a pittance. The fairs of Cornwall and Devon were our Madison Square Gardens and Albert Hall.

No one had heard of health and safety. In those days, £1 would buy the weekly groceries. Far more people worked on the land, or indeed, underneath it than today. Chapels were full, but thank

God, so too were the travelling fairs. Our role was to entertain. And amidst the deafening music, the boozers and the painted ladies stood Mickey Kiely.

He knew his audience, their moods and their backgrounds. He would stand, elegantly and impeccably dressed in a navy blue evening suit, often complimenting the towns and populations of Penzance, Launceston or Bodmin. He praised their menfolk in particular, especially if he spotted some legless farm labourers. "A county of real men, to challenge my men," he would implore, and as the crowd surged forward, he would pick on individuals. "You sir! You with that lovely lady on your arm. Is she really yours? Prove it! You look a man handy enough to defend yourself. What about it, sir? Show the young lady what you are made of."

It would only take one and, then, quite a few would follow. The later the hour, the drunker they were – lambs to the slaughter, more brawn and beer than brain, and certainly innocents into the arms of villains. Kiely was the master of exploitation... or rather deception and skulduggery.

The fighters would then, after insulting everybody within reasonable earshot, begin using intricate, delicate steps with ropes. All you could hear was the tap-tap rhythm of their toes, and the grunts and hissing breath of the fighters punching the heavy bag. The side-stake fighters – the real stars of the show – always used the speedball to demonstrate their quick reflexes and timing. Meanwhile Kiely was just as fast with the tongue, praising, goading, challenging. We would then be paraded individually before the masses. It was the same routine wherever we went. Three boxers in dressing gowns and three wrestlers alongside in leotards.

We would look mean and begin taunting the crowd, pointing towards some of the passing lads and shouting, "Come up here, you wimp," or "What are you doing with that faggot, lady?" Then the music was stopped. Invariably it was Val Doonican's 'Butterfly of Love'. Don't ask me why – it was Mickey's show. Then, the real 'sell' would begin.

"Ladies and gentlemen, my name is Mickey Kiely, your television sports personality. First of all, let me tell you how honoured my fighters feel to be allowed to be here in Bodmin to display some of the time-honoured intricacies of the martial arts. Bodmin is one of the jewels in the English crown. Behind me are some of the finest boxers and wrestlers in Europe today – magnificent specimens, ready and willing to take on all challengers. They are also fair fighters – I do not have any counterfeits. They are all genuine, and if the statements I make are found to be untrue, I will personally donate £1,000 to a local charity of your choice... If you have the courage to face one of them I will give you £5, but only if you can last three, just three, minute rounds with an opponent of your choice. Should you defeat one of them, the prize will be £20."

Twenty pounds in those days was the equivalent of two months' work on a nearby farm – a handsome enticement. Incidentally, I do not think any charity ever benefited. "So, good men of Bodmin! Come along. Do I have any challengers?"

Two hands would shoot up immediately. Two young lads, who had already spent a week's wages on beer that afternoon, would step up, waving to the crowd, hoping to win their bus fare home. They would be easy prey, but Kiely was not finished with his selling pitch.

"Give these brave sons of England your support. And where are you two lads from?" he'd ask. "We are both Bodmin men, born and bred, sir." The reply was accompanied once again by a huge cheer from the awaiting throng. "Are there anymore brave Bodmin men out there?" Kiely would ask, knowing that he might get a few more shows out of the night. "And which one of my fighters, boxers or wrestlers, will you take on, sirs," they'd be asked.

"I'll take that fungus-faced dick over there, and give him a good hidin'," the first one would say, much to the delight of the increasing crowd. "And you?"

"That bearded fat git... I'll wrestle 'im!"

One of my roles in those early days was to roam the crowds, spotting potential strong challengers. It would not do to have one of our own defeated. Serious potential challengers were called 'Gs' – genuine challengers – and Kiely would avoid calling them up until the last show of the night. The early show would feature youngsters, much the worse for drink, and would be mere fodder for my seasoned fellow travellers. There could be nine shows a day if the fairs were well attended, but the 'Gs' were kept back until the late hours. Kiely would make provision for them later. There was always one: "I'll fight the bloody lot of them. My name is Harry Hatfield as many around here would know. I've had five pints and I'm just in the mood to knock down a few men." Just the kind of challenger Kiely wanted.

"Right, sir," without changing his tone. "You will have the pick of the bunch. So what about taking on the masked man, Doctor Death?"

"I'll take off his head and his bloody mask," the challenger would shout and the cheers would in turn double the crowd, and the queues for half-crown tickets would lengthen.

"Right, sir, come with me and we'll get you changed for the fight."

"I'll fight as I am, and still knock him down."

"Sorry, but we have to obey Queensbury rules," Kiely would explain, as the challenger was shown to the caravan at the back of the tent. In the caravan, the challenger would be instructed by the referee to take off all his clothes, but invariably the underpants would stay on, until he was told that they would have to come off too – Queensbury rules! There would be protests, but with a packed tent waiting, no challenger would want to back off; most of them had enough beer inside them not to have a care anyway. The shorts provided would have an elastic waistband, which was far too loose for the challenger. And into the ring he would enter, with huge vocal approval from the local crowd.

The bell would ring and the booth fighter would immediately rush his opponent with a flurry of punches, forcing the challenger to put up his hands to protect himself. The loosely fitting trunks would drop. If the challenger didn't turn away and head for the caravan immediately, he would certainly spend the next uncomfortable few minutes more concerned about his falling trunks than the opponent in front of him. The fight would be over in seconds. There were a hundred Harry Hatfields to be had.

Each ring had a 'neutral' corner, though there was nothing neutral about it. The ring floor was made up of one-inch plyboards which overlapped the iron structure of the ring by twelve inches. However, in the neutral corner the boards would have been cut to nine inches. So, whenever a fighter was guided to this area, he would immediately suspect that there was a hole in the ring. Most would look down and that momentary distraction would be enough. It would be curtains for the challenger. These were the Queensbury or possibly Kiely's rules of the jungle. Round times were shortened or lengthened according to our progress against the challengers. We were told to 'carry' the weaker opponents for at least two rounds, to make a show of things.

In the unlikely event of a challenger giving one of our boys a really hard time, Kiely would instruct the referee to check the gloves at the end of a round. The referee would walk to the opponent's corner and ask him to present his gloves. The examination was seemingly thorough, and the gloves were eventually given the OK. So off he would go to the opposite corner to check the gloves of the booth fighter. Pushing his chest close to the fighter's gloves he would extract a razor blade, taped with Elastoplast, with one sharp corner showing. With a quick slash, he could create a four-inch gap in the right hand glove and then pull out the horsehair, which in those days was used as padding. Once this was exposed, the horsehair became seriously damaging to the opponent. Naturally, he made a meal of proclaiming that the gloves were OK. The next thing the challenger knew about the world was a barrage of blows to the head, blood flowing everywhere from deep cuts, and the fight was over. Of course it was corrupt and bent, but never orchestrated. The challengers were there for the taking. They were our livelihood.

The ladies next door were also making a living, and there was a close bond between the booth and strippers' hall. They were not the only ones on the fairground prostituting their bodies for monetary gain – we were too. And behind the face paint and rouge they were steely characters. We shared lives, laughs and beds. And more than once some of them were enlisted to help in the booth, by wearing next to nothing – an obvious distraction to any challenger.

By day, Kiely would teach us new moves. Not that the likes of my fellow travellers, Gordon Corbett and Harry Roberts could be taught anything, but the sixteen-year-old Peter Northey from Plymouth and I were keen disciples. Although I had been in the forces and had had brief spells as a football player and manager, I knew that I had to make a go of it in my new profession. I had little else to offer in terms of skill or knowledge. There was no alternative but to stick with this wrestling booth game. But I nearly quit – out of shame.

On a quiet night, when the number of challengers was low, we would have to fight each other on Mickey Kiely's travelling show. It was always a mismatch, since Gordon and Harry had been around for some time and Peter and I were learning the trade. There was no disgrace in losing to experienced exponents. But I knew that worse was to follow. Total humiliation, and I hated every minute of it. Kiely would wave Gordon's hand in the air, and I would lower my head. "Ladies and gentlemen, your winner tonight is the official area Heavyweight Champion Gordon Corbett. Your loser, and I am sure you will agree, a game loser from the Rhondda valley in south Wales – Orig Williams. Ladies and gentlemen, as most of you will be aware, the rules of boxing and wrestling in booths prohibits any payment whatsoever to be made to the loser in any contest. It is a sad, but a true fact. So, as a gesture to the extraordinary courage displayed by this young Welshman, we are going to come amongst you tonight with a hat for nubbins. I will add that the only reason this boy is in Cornwall tonight is because he lost his father in a pit accident in Tonypandy and he is the only family member who is earning a crust. Any pennies we can gather together will go to his grieving mother who is looking after his two brothers and two sisters in Wales. Tonight we saw what a tough little fighter he is, and he will have to be, to survive in this business. So, please give generously for the youngster and his family back in Wales." It was total bullshit!

But, I lowered my head and shuffled through the paltry

audience with cap in hand. I barely looked up. I was totally ashamed and I hated Kiley for placing me in this position. I was begging for a living... and I wasn't from Tonypandy anyway! If they knew in Ysbyty Ifan, or ever got to know, that I was walking around a tent in Cornwall begging for money, what would they say? Something like, "told you nothing good would come of that boy," perhaps? The next bout would be announced, and that was my signal to put away the cap, and give Kiely the nubbins. I suppose, being the newcomer, this ritual was my responsibility, but what else could I do? I had no other career. However, worse was to come.

Mickey Kiely, a showman of great talent was completely corrupt; he would always chase the last buck, and if there was any slack in the system, he would take action to rectify matters. His was a great tutelage. His travelling tour started in Cornwall on Good Friday and would finish, having stopped at all the good fairs, on the Town Moor in Newcastle in October. With at least four shows a night, little wonder that wrestlers and boxers came and went. I knew that I had to stay on, no matter what. One day, Kiely asked to see me. I entered the caravan and saw Kiely sitting surrounded by piles of money. "Orig, I need to have a serious discussion with you. Do you like this job or not?"

"Absolutely, yes indeed, sir," I replied. I always called everybody sir in those days, especially if I suspected trouble.

"Well, let me tell you," Kiely said, leaning forward. "You are a good fighter, a fine boxer, and you pick things up very quickly." So far so good, I thought.

"But Mother of God," shouted Kiely, "you are no bloody good at picking up nubbins. And what is more, the other boys are complaining about you! So what is wrong with you?"

"I just don't like it, sir." I spluttered. "It's just like begging."

"Begging?" Kiely was angry. "Begging, my arse." He got up. "How can you think it's begging when you have entertained all those suckers for one hell of a fight?"

"It's in the Bible, sir... in the Good Book... you shouldn't beg!" That was it.

"I don't know where or how you were brought up, but the

Good Book and its words don't have any meaning or worth around here – God help me," he roared. He lit a cigar, and blew the smoke in my direction. I suspected that this was the end of my short career. "The truth of the matter is that the lads who go on with you are getting to the point where they don't want to go on with you, because when they do, they get lousy nubbins. It is their bonus, remember, and they have got wives and families to feed. Those nubbins make a huge difference."

I knew that every one of the gang was paid £1 a fight, win or lose, so they were not totally relying on my begging act. Kiely wasn't finished. "I tell you what," he said, "You've got three days to get your act together on the nubbins. And I don't want to hear about begging again. Do you understand? Three days, and unless there is an improvement, you will be back on your way to the Rhondda valley, or wherever you bloody come from."

"Ysbyty Ifan," I replied.

"Get out!" he shouted. It did the trick. The boys took me out for a drink, since I had been visibly shaken by Kiely's tirade. "You told Kiely that you were begging?" asked Peter. "That took more balls than getting into any ring."

In three days I turned into a credible thespian and beggar. When the cap went out amongst the crowd, I still shuffled, but told the punters we were a poor family, and the kids back home were starving. Suddenly there were two-bob pieces, even half-crowns in the cap, and the weight of the nubbins brought a smile to Kiely's face. But later in life I never begged, never shuffled. If I asked for or wanted something, I looked a person in the eye and stretched the truth.

Something else happened to increase our wages and punters as well. ITV's wrestling viewing figures on Saturday afternoons continued to rise and armchair viewing had made household names of Jackie Paulo, Billy Two Rivers and Big Daddy. As we trundled, town by town, fair by fair towards Newcastle – our final destination for the season – Kiely was at it every night. His drive and enthusiasm was extraordinary. And he made full use of the increasing popularity of television wrestling

"Come on in boys. Have a go at the only man to floor Jackie

Pallo at the Albert Hall." Not one of us, I don't think, had ever been to or even seen the Albert Hall, let alone met Mr 'TV' Pallo. Suddenly though, we were catapulted into fake TV stardom – we were British or area wrestling champions overnight, or the 'country's next wrestling sensation'. I was learning at the foot of the master. Charming one minute, challenging the next. He was a salesman, a manipulator of people – their egos, fears and ambitions. But, above all else, he was a first-class businessman. I watched him, like an attentive pupil at school on his first day. Had I been given this education before becoming a football manager, I might have aspired to greater things. But at this moment in time, I was lodged between the Wall of Death and the lady strippers in Bodmin.

Mickey looked after us and although we slept rough, we were always fed properly. What we did in our spare time was none of his business – the strippers' next door also contributed to our education. Later on, if I knew a wrestler had been through and survived the Kiely academy, I knew that I had a good one. Kiely's graduates included Freddie Mills, Randolph Turpin and Jimmy Wilde, and a few hundred more. Ironically, as wrestling began to flourish on ITV, Mickey also introduced more wrestling on his tours, and this is where the likes of Roy Bull Davies, Pat Roach, Johnny Kincaid and Klondyke Kate honed their skills.

Later, long after leaving the Kiely academy, I became friendly with another legendary fairground promoter. Ronnie Taylor was the grandson of a bare-knuckle mountain fighter and had inherited the family travelling booth which travelled to all the fairs throughout Wales and beyond. Four generations of the Taylor family fought in the booth and Ronnie regularly featured female boxers – when he could find them. There was nothing Ronnie would like more than to sit and tell us the tales of when the likes of Tommy Farr, Cliff Curvis and the Turpin brothers used to grace his booth and, in particular, when he was visited by Mohammed Ali. Both of us would sit and wax about our fellow countryman Jimmy Wilde, one-time fly-weight champion of the world, who began his pugilistic life in Jack Skarratt's booths in Tylorstown in the Rhondda valley. Here he was, a sickly lad of six stones eight pounds, fighting boys who were two stones heavier. In his first competition, he knocked three of them out and won a coffee set. As a twelve-year-old he was already working underground, but one day, at the booths at Aberdare, he fought sixteen opponents, all at different weights, and knocked out fifteen of them. One lad managed to go three rounds with him. He was given £1 and Wilde was rewarded with £1 10/- for the whole day. When he won the Seven Stone World Championships, his prize money – a share of the gate – was £8 and 13 shillings! And when he was defeated by Peter Herman in his penultimate fight, the fight lasted seventeen rounds! Ronnie and I could go on forever about the booths and those who fought and survived in them. Kiely and Taylor were priceless legends.

CHAPTER 6

Bholu's Pakistan

I WAS DESTINED TO meet and become a lifelong friend of Akram Bholu and his wrestling brothers. It must have been written somewhere that a man from the hinterland of Ysbyty Ifan would inevitably meet a Punjabi man, who was revered by his nation and people. He was the head of a wrestling family dynasty, a descendant of the Great Gama Pehalwan – a legend of Pakistani and Indian wrestling. Together, Akram Bholu and his brothers – Aslam, Goga, Azam and Jahir – had a hand in just about everything that moved in Pakistan, and I mean everything. Akram Bholu made Al Capone seem like an indecisive pauper. The path to his friendship, though, was bewildering, a long and often painful journey, and always surprising.

"Religion?" asked the immigration official on my arrival at Karachi airport.

"Welsh Calvinistic Methodist," I replied promptly, wondering why on earth he wanted to know. "Never heard of it," he replied. I immediately felt sorry for the man. How could he not have heard of Welsh Methodism? Had he not sung 'Bread of Heaven'? "Are you a Christian or a Muslim?"

"I have no idea, I am just a Methodist." The man with the folder was losing patience, and so was I, but I had never been questioned like this before. Mrs Davies in Sunday school had told us in no uncertain terms that there was one God, and that he was a Methodist, and that was that, no further questions asked. "Do you believe in God or Allah, then?"

"God, of course," I replied, having little or no idea, at that time, who or what Allah was.

"Then you are a Christian," and, as he entered my reply on his folder, I thought of Mrs Davies, who would have to be questioned about this. It had been a trying, restless fourteen-hour flight from London, via Stuttgart and teetotal Dubai, and it had given me ample time to question the wisdom of accepting Chief Thunderbird's invitation to fly to and fight in Pakistan.

Chief Thunderbird's real name was Ben Wojkowski. He was tall and dark skinned, with an Indian headdress of tomahawks that would not have looked out of place in a John Wayne film. Ben's story was, however, far more dramatic than any celluloid fiction. During the Second World War, Ben, then a seventeen-year-old boy, was sitting in a cinema in his native Warsaw, when German soldiers entered searching for Polish Jews. Frightened, Ben escaped through a toilet window, and penniless, he began a remarkable trek to Britain on foot. He was multilingual, an extremely intelligent man and had become well acquainted and well connected in the wrestling world. Chief Thunderbird really impressed me. He had approached a bunch of us in our caravan at the end of a summer season of booth wrestling. None of us had any work for the winter months and Ben said he had been asked to take two heavyweight wrestlers to Pakistan for a month. I had no idea where Pakistan was. Prestatyn and Preston? No problem. Pakistan? However, I volunteered, and I was on my way. This was going to be my first overseas visit, and also my first experience of air travel.

Chief Thunderbird had promised riches far beyond the pay nights around the British halls and summer resorts, where £10 a week was the usual payment. Thunderbird said that two heavyweights could earn £100 each week, with food and lodgings thrown in. The average weekly wage in Britain at that time was £3, so the proposal represented a handsome reward.

Although I had travelled around football grounds, fairgrounds and RAF camps and had about a year's experience of the wrestling halls, I was a total innocent abroad, and was about to prove it. Pakistani Airlines had none of the comforts that go with modern-day flying, but it mattered little in the excitement of it all. I just could not comprehend being on the tarmac one minute, and flying over London the next. Yes, I was *that* green, nervous and uncomfortable. I tried to engage a fellow passenger in conversation – a lady in a sari and wearing a veil. Despite repeated attempts I had no reply, merely a stoic stare. She was deaf, I thought, or couldn't speak English. So I turned to my right and had a chat with a bearded gentleman, who lost no time at all in telling me that female Pakistani Muslims would not engage in any kind of a conversation with strangers. That put paid to any thoughts of how we were going to entertain ourselves on arrival.

By the time we had hopscotched to Karachi and survived an alcohol-free flight, immigration, the interrogation and a chaotic search for our luggage, it was time to meet and greet our host and agent, Salim Sadiq – all twenty-five stone of him. If this was the promoter, I thought, what size would their wrestlers be? Once the salutations were completed, we thought we would head for the hotel and then to bed, since neither of us had slept since leaving London.

The terminal was a sea of people and intense activity. And this was four o'clock in the morning! Suddenly, we became aware of a large group of photographers hurtling towards us. I said to Thunderbird that someone important must be arriving, but lo and behold they began taking photographs of us, and asking *us* questions. "Who are you? What are your names? Can you spell Orig? Where do you come from? What do you think of Pakistan? Have you heard of the Pakistani wrestlers? Have you heard of the Bholu brothers?"

We were pushed and shoved into a VIP lounge for an impromptu press conference, and the questions kept coming. This was my first ever press conference. We'd not experienced anything like this in Lancashire or Rhyl! "We are very tired," I told someone who looked official. "Can we go to bed? Where is our hotel?"

It was another two days before we saw our promoter, Salim, again. He arrived at our hotel dressed like a colonial white hunter, wearing a large white shirt and trousers, with the air of ruling imperialism. "Pack your belongings," he said, "we are off to Lahore for the wrestling. The plane leaves in an hour."

The plane to Lahore was a museum piece. It struggled to get into the air. I was beginning to learn a fundamental lesson about Pakistan life. Always expect the unexpected. The short journey to

Lahore was an hour and a half flight. And again, at Lahore airport, there was a mighty media throng, repeating the questions we had heard at Karachi. But there were also thousands of others there to meet us. Flowers were draped around our necks, our backs were patted, but most people just stared – all of which was very bewildering. Salim explained that no white wrestlers had ever been to Pakistan, and people wanted to see us. But we could not have anticipated his next move.

Salim explained that such was the excitement of the people, he wanted to put on a bit of a parade for them and for us, but basically it was all promotion for him and his work. Lesson two in Pakistan: everyone is an operator with an angle. We were not prepared for his marketing ploy. Two camels were produced from a street corner. He beckoned two small boys, the camel jockeys, to come forward and instruct us on how best to climb on board. I had never been on a Rhyl donkey, let alone a camel! Thunderbird was not amused.

We all protested, but to no avail, and three hours later, in the increasing heat of the day, we were still on board, weaving through rickshaws, bikes, cattle and chickens, chasing kids and chaotic traffic. Salim was thrilled. We were dumbfounded and aching, as every bone in our bodies protested. Then, at last, we were taken to the Mehran Hotel, expecting bed and a rest. No chance.

Once inside, we were directed into a large room, where some fifty people had gathered and were seated in a semicircle. In their midst were five large men, looking solemn but also fierce. These were the Bholu brothers. It suddenly dawned on Ben and I that this was why we were the first white wrestlers to venture into these lands. There was not a smile or gesture of welcome from them to us. Salim addressed the gathering in Urdu. He had a very attentive audience. Occasionally, all eyes turned to us. Eventually, he translated for our benefit. "I have explained to the Bholu brothers and to the press that you are here as 'representatives' of the British Empire, and that you are here to teach us a lesson!" Thank you Salim! The Bholus did not require any encouragement. We both wondered what had possessed us to come to this country. "Food?" asked Salim. "What would you like?"

We were beyond food. "Would you like chicken?" he asked. "Yes, some chicken would be fine," we replied out of politeness.

"And how many would you like?"

"Just one each would be fine," we replied. Salim laughed. "The Bholu brothers eat six chickens each, every meal! And Akram, who is your opponent, once ate a whole sheep for a meal, and drank a gallon of goats' milk afterwards."

This was a wind-up merchant of the first order I thought. But, I had a niggling doubt that there might have been a small element of truth in this story. It was too late to worry now, I would find out soon enough.

A few hours later, after limited sleep, I was on my way with Thunderbird and Salim to the stadium. The streets were packed with people walking towards it, and you could hear the shouts of 'Infidel' and 'English pigs'. Suddenly, we saw the stadium – a massive oval cricket ground. It had a crowd capacity of 120,000. Wembley was midget-sized compared with this, and this was where a white Welsh Methodist Christian was about to be fed to the Muslim lions. Salim smiled. This was a big payday for any promoter. A hundred pounds a week with food and lodging – we were the biggest suckers in town. There was not a spare seat, tree or roof in or outside the stadium. I paced up and down in the changing room and went to the toilet about a hundred times. The noise outside was deafening and frightening. My fight was the last on the bill – something which I have always hated. The wait seemed like an eternity.

But, suddenly, there he stood on the opposite side of the ring. Serene and majestic with the green and white flag of Pakistan draped around his shoulders – all six foot three inches of him. Akram had an air of invincibility, a presence, and I now believed that he had eaten a whole sheep for a meal. He was undefeated. I told myself, "Orig, I think you've made a big mistake here, boy."

The referee called us over. Akram was bigger than I had first thought. "Ten five-minute rounds, you understand? One fall or a knock-out and you win."

"What about submissions?" I asked in all innocence.

"Submissions? Submissions?" he replied. "What are those? We do not have them here. Akram is fighting for Allah, and will not, as you say, submit. First, he will die – or you will." Yes, I thought, this is bullshit – but I had a niggling doubt.

Allah Madhat. Allah Madhat. Allah Madhat. Aki. Aki. Aki.

It was incessant. Christ, I wanted the toilet again. Sportsmen will tell you of jelly-like legs and pumping hearts when confronted by challenges. I was a wreck by now: bladder, legs, arms, brain – the lot.

As soon as the fight started, I realised that Akram was not only large, but far stronger than me. If I was to survive, which seemed highly doubtful at the time, guile and speed would have to be constant companions. He was cautious himself, since he had never fought anyone outside Pakistan and the moves of the professional world were unknown to him. But he grew in confidence and began to dominate, sending the crowd into a chorus of frenzied approval with every blow.

Aki. Aki. Aki.

By round three, I knew I was in trouble as he continually lined me up with blows.

They were systematically weakening me and both he and the crowd knew it. To his fans, here was a hero punishing a white man from Britain, the one-time oppressors and occupiers, and each blow was a blow for the injustices meted out by the empire. This was revenge; this was political. To a Welshman, who didn't believe in the damn empire anyway, it was also painful. The little red dragon flag that I carried everywhere looked limp on the corner post. By the end of the third round, I was being pulverised. It would take something exceptional to turn this one around.

At the beginning of the fourth round, I gathered all reserves of energy and strength and lunged across the ring as soon as the bell had gone, and drop kicked Akram on the chin. It was a superb execution of the kick, the best I ever delivered. He went down like a sack, and the crowd went silent. Methodist 1 – Muslim 0.

But my delight was short-lived. Akram recovered, and the tidal lashings I had suffered were now taking their toll. I could feel the energy disappear, and I knew that the tank was empty. With great effort, I got both his arms behind my back. Suddenly he dived forward, kicking out with his legs in a mule fashion and planting both his feet with great ferocity under my chin. I didn't see it coming, and have never seen it better executed. I remember the count of ten and out.

I struggled to come around. My two seconds (that is, the corner men who held the towels, etc.) were too busy dancing around the ring with a Pakistani flag.

Allah Madhat. Allah Madhat. Aki. Aki. Aki.

The crowd were delirious. I remember my grandmother telling me that God worked in mysterious ways. She was right, since I do not think that Allah or his supporters, had I won, would have allowed me out of the ring, stadium or country that night. A diplomatic defeat, I thought. Yet, I had also gained the respect of Akram and his brothers, which, in the long term, would prove to be highly beneficial and certainly 'educational'.

The Bholu family had amassed a large fortune from wrestling in Amritsar, but in 1946, like so many hundreds of thousands of Muslims, they were forced to leave India when the British decided on a religious partition of India and the establishment of Pakistan. Families, including the Bholus, were ordered to leave by foot, and take with them whatever worldly wealth they had on the back of a single cow. That was all that was allowed. But, not the Bholu family. They enlisted ten poor Muslims, hired them and their cattle for their own use and possession, yet still left behind a considerable fortune. They settled in Lahore, and it wasn't long before this desolate area chosen by the British to accommodate the Muslims began flourishing with Himalayan irrigation water, and with it the rekindling of the Bholu family fortunes.

Wrestling was popular and profitable there, but in the chaotic upheaval and development of the new country, so too was crime. The Bholus, like so many, took advantage of every opportunity, legal or otherwise. Akram, the eldest brother and son of Bholu, was a superb negotiator: a rogue operator, entrepreneur, but principally, an extremely 'respectable' gangster. He had little command of English and could not write, but in time he controlled regions, towns, property and people. The Bholus and various relatives had very many brothels and control of the infamous diamond market and stores of Lahore.

In the market, he once offered me the services of a genuine virgin, as if he were selling me Tupperware. And this in front of a woman who I assumed to be her mother. The street-corner beggars were all in his pocket, since he allowed them to be there through his own license agreement. Begging was an accepted profession, especially for the impoverished young – self-inflicted broken bones in children were common. It gave the beggars credibility. The Bholus could arrange anything and everything. There were few areas where they and their relatives did not have influence, which in turn became affluence. Gambling dens, drugs, prostitution – they were all ruled by the descendants of the Great Gama Pehalwan, of who Akram Bholu was one. I came to accept that in Pakistan anything was possible, but everything had a price. It was the only way out of adversity for some. What Akram Bholu wanted, he got. Politicians were petrified of his power and this enhanced his popularity and status. But he was, or seemed to be, incredibly generous also. Akram Bholu was a brilliant manipulator of men and situations.

And, yet, not one of the brothers could read nor write. I knew that since I had to sign forms for them at airports and at any other official places. As young children, their destiny was the wrestling world, following in the family's footsteps. And so there was no need for education or schooling. They were taught that to survive they had to successful, to be streetwise, to be second to none. And they had passed those exams with flying colours.

My introduction to the Bholu family had been a painful one. Akram was now being hailed as the conquering hero in the stadium – the master of the infidel. Yet, this was the beginning of a great friendship with the Bholu brothers. We left Lahore and fought in a few other places, drawing huge and enthusiastic partisan crowds. We were being paid well, since we were travelling with Bholu 'royalty'. Then a chance meeting in Turkey, on our homeward journey with another incoming wrestler, was to change our lives, at least for a few years.

King Kong, or Emil Kovacks, a multilinguist originally from Budapest, had been around for a long time – so he knew his way around the wrestling circuit. He could not believe that we were returning home after so much success. "You could wrestle in this part of the world for the rest of your life and make a fortune without having to go to the same venue twice," he claimed. Salim, the Pakistan promoter was still with us, and was an attentive listener. He would not or could not leave this precious 'marketing ticket for life' alone. We talked and a deal was struck, which naturally delighted Salim. We would stay in this part of the world – Thunderbird, Emil and a Welsh Methodist – for £150 a week, take it or leave it, with all expenses thrown in on top. Salim, who had seen what an attraction we were was most accommodating, which made me a little suspicious that perhaps, once again, we were being taken for a ride. But, the money was good!

We stayed for eighteen months and were joined by other wrestlers. We roamed around from show to show, from culture to culture throughout Pakistan, Turkey, Sri Lanka and Sierra Leone. We had enormous audiences, and Salim's smile grew wider than his bulging wallet. But international politics soon intervened. Relationships between India and Pakistan deteriorated, and a war between the countries was imminent. And, to be honest, I was feeling homesick.

There is a word in Welsh called *hiraeth*. It means a longing for home and this fellow was suffering from an acute bout of *hiraeth*. I hadn't been home for two years. I wanted to see some green mountains. It sounds silly, perhaps, but it was true. So I went home.

Salim rang me a few times, asking me to return. His motive was obvious: he had never experienced anything as productive as the white wrestling travelling circus. Eventually his persistence paid off, and I said I would return, but he had an additional request. Could I bring another heavyweight with me? The Pakistanis had a great regard for big men. "No problem there," I told him, "I have the very man."

Klondyke Bill was five foot ten inches tall, but weighed more than thirty stones. He'd been spotted by Don Robinson, a very wealthy man from the north-east, who was a Yorkshire TV director, and also director of Scarborough Football Club. Klondyke, or Gordon Lythe, to give him his real name, was a bit of a passive character – a bit of a loner and mild-mannered and had only had a few unconvincing bouts. Robinson asked me to take him on and train him.

Because of his size, Klondike had been the target of a fair amount of leg pulling, especially in his day job as a grocery assistant in Melton. So he had taken up judo, where his size was of advantage. We had become good friends on the British circuit, working and training together – so I knew he was the man for the job. He was a good traveller, a reader and not a flamboyant noisy type at all. He had a heart of gold, and was especially kind to kids – always carrying a bag of jelly babies with him. Wherever he went, Klondyke was the subject of great interest – not all of it complimentary, until people realised he was a wrestler. He was enormous, there was no question about that, and his huge stomach was rock hard. All the UK wrestlers would testify to that. Despite his size, he was incredibly mobile and he also had a quick brain, which in wrestling is a major plus. Salim was delighted. He did not think that there was such a huge man in the whole of Pakistan. I urged him to tell his press contacts that Klondyke was coming.

I seem to have spent a lifetime booking two seats for large wrestlers on planes. On arrival in Karachi, there was a massive turn out to greet the thirty-stone wrestler from Britain. I am not sure what they expected, but they were stunned into silence. Salim had acquired a weighing scale from somewhere, and Klondyke clambered aboard. Round went the needle, reaching the 452-pound mark. There was an instantaneous round of appreciative applause. The picture of Klondyke on the scales would make the morning papers. But, so did another photograph.

There were no awaiting camels this time. Salim had a pony and trap waiting outside the terminal. The mighty crowd followed watching Klondyke struggle to get on board. He had hardly placed a foot on the steps up to the trap when all of a sudden the lightweight pony was propelled upwards, airborne, kicking air and helpless. That picture made all the front pages too. Publicity was secured and whatever Klondyke did during the next few days was duly snapped for posterity.

He became an overnight overweight sensation. Wherever we went, a mighty crowd followed. We were wined and dined, clothed and feted by shops, restaurants, tailors and shoe makers – all of them wanting their establishments in the papers for being associated with this great man from Yorkshire. Klondyke loved every minute of it, and probably ended up with 452 suits, shirts and shoes!

News of the Klondyke sensation reached East Pakistan, or Bangladesh as it is now called. The president of the country had heard of the arrival of the wrestlers and had contacted Bholu – the man who could fix anything. The president wanted a wrestling show and was obviously very keen to have us, since he offered Akram and ourselves a stadium for free. Akram was not overly impressed by this offer and wanted to know its capacity. He was told it would hold a 100,000 people. He didn't bat an eye, and begrudgingly said it would only just do. A hundred thousand! Three hundred would have been a good home gate at Nantlle Vale. He would accept the free stadium offer, he said, if the president would provide twelve airline tickets as well. I could not believe my ears. We had the revenue of a potential 100,000 crowd and this man was haggling for airline tickets with the president of a country!

They arrived three days later, and we were off to East Pakistan. I knew our destiny was in the hands of a master haggler! East Pakistan was a pitifully poor and dirty country. There had been areas in and around Karachi and Lahore that had defied description in terms of filth and squalor, but this was a living hell, fit for no one. Dacca was an over-populated virtual cesspit, yet, on the day of the big event, thousands came by any means of transport available. There were more people hanging onto the trains than riding inside. It was a massive crowd. But how could they afford to pay? Most of the sea of thousands didn't look as if they had eaten a meal for weeks.

The president arrived to sit on four sofas reserved for himself and his guests. It was to be a day-long affair since there were twenty-five amateur fights to settle in an extensive warm-up programme. As usual, we drew lots to determine the order of fights. My adopted name Orig Pehalwan (Orig Wrestler) was first out, and the second name drawn was that of Jahir, the Tiger – champion of East Pakistan. I was in for a tough one. This was a man with a point to prove in front of his home crowd – and his president.

Just as in my first fight in Pakistan, my opponent was the stronger man – that became quite obvious after our first tangles. Jahir was also quick and, much to the delight of the loud partisan crowd, he easily won the first four rounds. Surprisingly, however, for a champion, he wasn't that fit, and his moves were limited and at times obvious. The longer the fight progressed, I thought, the better my chances. And so it proved, as Jahir tired and I won the remaining rounds. Try as I might, however, I could not floor him. The fight was declared a draw, a decision which neither the crowd nor I found disagreeable. Jahir jumped from the ring and ran straight to the president and kissed his shoes. He asked the president for a great favour. Could he have another opportunity of beating me? Logistically, it was impossible that night, since there were several other fights, including the much-awaited appearance of Klondike Bill, who dismissed Azam Bholu quite easily.

The president found himself in a dilemma. He had to be seen to be in a position of influence. Had he not been able to bring the white wrestlers to his country? How could he not grant the wrestling champion of East Pakistan his wish? But, he would have to negotiate with Bholu. I felt sorry for the president. We were due to fly back to Karachi in the morning, but the president asked Bholu if we could delay our departure for a couple of days and stage a re-match on the following Friday. Bholu asked for a few moments to consider and discuss. All of these details were announced to the crowd, who could not leave the stadium until the departure of the president. This was tense stuff indeed!

I had been learning a great deal from Akram Bholu, the negotiator and manipulator, but now it was my turn. Bholu approached Klondyke and myself with an interpreter and asked if we had any objection to prolonging our stay. "There is no way," I told him through the interpreter, "that we want to stay in this shit-hole, whatever the deal is." How that was translated I don't know. "Why?" asked Akram.

"Take a look around. These people can't afford to pay for another show."

"What if I gave you a percentage of the gate?"

"What gate? I have told you. They can't afford another show." I was warming to my role as negotiator at the feet of the master. I turned to the interpreter, who was also a solicitor.

"Tell Bholu that I respect him, and we are here as a gesture of that respect. If we are to stay, as he wishes, then our weekly pay will be doubled, and that the fight between me and Jahir will have a side stake of a thousand pounds – winner takes all." On hearing my response Bholu laughed loudly. "But you do not have a thousand pounds to put up," he said.

"I know that, and so do you," I replied. "But you have a thousand. And those are my terms."

He understood all right and he knew he was beaten. *Shwkira Pehalwan* (thank you, wrestler). The deal was done: the re-match would take place. It was announced to the awaiting crowd. There was a huge roar of approval. The president was pleased and the crowd left. Bholu treated me with a little more respect after that negotiation. But the re-match was given added significance. Here was the champion of East Pakistan against the champion of Wales, as I had already styled myself. I doubt if anyone in East Pakistan had heard of Wales. It didn't matter, I was a champion, and this was the decider.

On the night of the fight I realised I had made a mistake. I should have taken a percentage of the gate. There were even more people there than at the first night. It was an incredible sight. How today's Health and Safety of Grounds Act people would have coped, I have no idea. You couldn't have got a goat in there!

The contest with Jahir, much reported in miles of column inches in the press, was the last fight on the bill. How I hated waiting! Pacing around the room, I thought of the £1,000 stake, and what a fool I had been. A thousand pounds was a pittance against a percentage of the gate! I was that innocent. I could have bought two houses in Ysbyty Ifan! Thoughts of this and thoughts of that but, mainly, thoughts of what the hell was I doing here in the first place! It didn't help to see that the masses had returned to see the revenge fight. I had been out-thought by the master again! Another lesson learnt. Klondyke soon dispensed with his opponent, his reputation enhanced yet again. And eventually it was my turn.

I now knew what to expect from Jahir. He was strong but he had his limitations. The early rounds were predictable, with Jahir using his superior strength and I became something of a punch bag, being thrown around the ring like a newly sheared sheep. I allowed him ample opportunity to show his skills, without counterattacking. Jahir won the first five rounds comfortably, and was now brimming with confidence. The home support was ecstatic. They were expecting an early finish. That is why they had come. I spent some considerable time on the mat as Jahir delivered a downpour of blows. Down again, another count. By round six, the crescendo of noise from the crowd seemed to signal that the end was nigh as I went sprawling once again. The bell rang.

As soon as it rang again at the beginning of round seven I did a greyhound sprint across the ring and delivered a drop kick to Jahir's chin. It was timed to perfection and, as he fell, I knew that there would be no recovery. I had duped him into being over-confident and he had a lapse in concentration. He was counted out, as I knew he would be. The crowd were stunned, silent and disbelieving. I strode around the ring shouting "Wales for ever! Wales for ever!" How I wish there had been a *Daily Post* reporter there to record this triumph. Akram gave me the £1,000 side-stake on the return flight to Karachi. "Tell me," he said, "how were you so confident about beating Jahir?" I explained that at the first fight neither I nor Jahir had used our feet, certainly no

Ysbyty Ifan Primary School and the second from the left in the middle row is 'Mr Innocence'.

Pwllheli FC: I'm second from the right on the back row. Tarw Nefyn is first on the left on the same row with Tommy Jones standing next to him.

Nantlle Vale FC: I'm not in this picture; I can't remember why! Tarw Nefyn is second from the left on the back row.

THE FOOTBALL ASSOCIATION OF WALES
LIMITED

Patron:
H.M. THE QUEEN.

Telephone: 2425.

Telegrams: WELSOCCER, WREXHAM.

Secretary:
HERBERT POWELL, O.B.E.

**3 FAIRY ROAD,
WREXHAM.**

5th April, 1968.

Dear Sir,

    I have received your letter ....

dated ....1st April........, for which I thank you.

        The matter is receiving attention ~~noted~~

        Yours faithfully,

H. Powell

Secretary

I received many of these from Herbert Powell in the 1960s.

TWO PLAYERS S...

Bangor k.o. Nantlle in Challenge cup semi-final

BANGOR CITY 3. NANTLLE VALE 0

BANGOR City qualified to meet Holyhead Town

B in th
Challenge
over Nan
Monday

The gar
ending o
or's cen
and Nan
Thomas—
hour be
enes fo
As th
booing
dozens
the pi
near t
s h
minute
Bang
dash
for
which
league
the st
they
their
with t
Nan
Willie
well
held
mark
v for
nuet

Williams fined and suspended for 28 days

Nantlle Vale F.C. player-manager, Orig Williams has been suspended for 28 days from last Monday and fined £10 10s by a disciplinary Committee of the Welsh F.A. for striking an opponent during the Cookson Cup semi-final Nantlle Vale and

this
Na
first
had
Cook
falle
prov
cro'
Wre
leve
vere
the
ding
ame
the

ATGOFION AM 'NANTLLE FÊL'

Dewch yn ôl gyda mi i'r chwedegau a dechrau'r saithdegau i gae'r 'Fêl' pan oedd Orig yn chwaraewr-reolwr ar dîm y Dyffryn. Roedd ei ddyfodiad i'r Clwb yn ddigwyddiad o bwys, a bwrlwm a brwdfrydedd ymysg y boblogaeth. Roeddem ni'r plant yn edrych arno fel arwr o'r eiliadau cyntaf y troediodd y maes — roedd cael mynd i gae'r 'Fêl' i weld Orig yn chwarae yn goron ar bob penwythnos. Nid oherwydd ei fod yn chwaraewr mor ddawnus neu fedrus â llawer um o'i gwmpas, ond roedd 'na frwdfrydedd yno, ac yn fwy na dim roedd hwn yn gymeriad ar ei ben ei hun. Cymeriad yng nghanol criw o gymeriadau — a phob un ohonyn nhw'n Gymry Cymraeg naturiol o'r ardaloedd cyfagos.

Does gen i ddim co' i'r tîm ennill dim dan oruchwyliaeth Orig, na hyd yn oed dod yn agos at ennill dim byd chwaith, ond roedd 'na hwyl a sbort a sbri o'r mwyaf yr âi rhywun trwy'r clwydi.

Byddai Orig ac un neu ddau o'r chwaraewyr eraill wedi cyfarfod ychydig cyn y gêm yng Nghaffi Wil Rhos, ac yno, yn aml iawn, dros baned o goffi, y byddid yn trin a thrafod tactegau am y prawn. Gwnaem ninnau'r plant yn siŵr ein bod yn eistedd ar y bwrdd agosaf atynt fel y gallem ninnau gael clust i'r cyfrinachau.

"Idris, cer di i fyny am y gic gornel gynta, a hitia Pen Brwsh (athro celf oedd yn y gôl i Borthmadog bryd hynny) i mewn i'r gôl, mi af inna am y nesa."

A wir i chi, fel yna yn union y byddai hi yn ystod y gêm, ac Orig yng ngwir ddull yr ymgodymwr yn taflu'i hun, ei goesau gyntaf, am flaenwr y tîm arall o byddai'n mynnu mynd heibio iddo, eu clymu rownd ei ganol, a'i wasgu nes y byddai hwnnw fel sach o flawd ar y llawr. Pledio wedyn hefo'r dyfarnwr, a gwên fawr ar ei wyneb, nad oedd wedi gwneud dim nad oedd o fewn y rheolau. Byddai gŵr y siwt ddu ac Orig yn cael sgwrs fach yn aml iawn bob gêm, — ac weithiau âi'r chwarae'n chwerw a gwelid corff enfawr Orig yn troedio'n araf bach am gawod gynnar.

Byddai rhai ohonom yn mynd gyda'r tîm i'r gemau oddi cartref, ac yn fynych iawn teithiem gydag Orig yn ei Jaguar gwyn am Y Rhyl, Llandudno neu Flaenau Ffestiniog. Wedi cyrraedd, caem esgus gario'r bagiau i mewn, a thrwy hynny osgoi gorfod talu am fynediad i'r maes.

Wedi'r gêm, sgwrs a thrin a thrafod, ond waeth beth fyddai'r canlyniad — ac roedd 'na ganlyniadau trychinebus ambell i Sadwrn — roedd 'na rhyw ddireidi yn perthyn iddo, a chaem yr argraff mai'r chwarae oedd yn bwysig iddo ac nid yr ennill.

RHODRI GWYNN JONES

NANTLLE PLAYERS SUSPENDED

on
they packed B
mt.
SURPRISED

by Williams
when well placed and t

J.

---

were booked

NANTLLE VALE

22/10/67

Double trou... for Nantl...

BANGOR CITY 2. NANTLL...

it was double trouble for still
Vale in this game ag...
sday for not

NANTLLE PLAY SENT OFF

Nantlle team war... by referee

BANGOR U.C. 3. NANTLLE VALE

THE entire Nantlle Vale team were cal... side by referee D. A. Jones, of Per... draeth, early in the second half of th... League game and given a general warning...

Herald 8/11/88

NANTLLE BO... SENT OFF

QUEENSFERRY WANDERERS 3. NANTLLE VA...

NANTLLE'S player-manager Orig Willia... sent off in the 71st minute of...
Hawarden...

16/1/70

FIVE PLAY... BOOKE...

PRESTATYN 2, NANTLLE V...

Herald 6/2/70

Orig sent ... in fourth mi...

BANGOR CITY 2. NANTLLE VALE

NANTLLE Vale player-manager Or... played the shortest match of his lo... g career at Bangor on Saturday, whe... Williams of Caernarvon... ters after on... 'od y chwaraewr o Nantlle yn gapelwr... selog, yn mynychu'r sgiat ac yn athro... ysgol Sul. Mae'n rhaid fod golwg o sioc... ac anghredinaeth lwyr ar wyneb... cyhuddiedig. Collodd ei achos.

Wrth gofio'r Orig Williams a fu'r... rheolwr tîm pêl-droed Nantlle, rhai... atal y gwamalu am ychydig, a tha... teyrnged iddo am gadw pêl-droed... ardal gyda thîm o Gym...

Richard Morris Jones ac El Bandito

Yr hyn yr ydw i yn ei gofio fwyaf am 'y gêm gyntaf honno a chwaraeais gydag ef i'r 'Vale', ydi bygythiad Orig pan geisiodd rhyw asgellwr fwy annwybodus na'i gilydd fy nghicio. Wedi iddo gydio yn y creadur, ac egluro wrtho sut welyd-au oedd yn Ysbyty Môn ac Arfon Bangor, cefais lonydd perffaith am weddill y gêm.

Theatr oedd y cae pêl-droed iddo fel y sgwâr reslo erbyn heddiw.

Ciciau cornel oedd maes ymchwil arbennig Orig. Pan fyddai cic i Nantlle byddai Orig yno, yn neidio i fyny ac i lawr yn y cwrt cosbi yn disgwyl am y croesiad, ac yn gweiddi am y dyfarnwr, "Watch him ref, hey ref, he's pushing, ref" (am ryw reswm Saeson oedd y rhan fwyaf o'r dyfarnwyr). Byddai ambell i ddyfarnwr gwan wedi drysu'n lân. A mwy nag unwaith gwelais Orig yn syrthio'n druenus o boenus gan waeddi "REF". Y gwir ydi mai anamal iawn y gweithiodd y stŵr, ond roedd Orig, a gweithiodd y ddrama. Theatr

Cofiaf 'funud o dawelwch' er parch i goffadwriaeth Herbert Powell, Ysgrifennydd Cymdeithas Pêl-droed Cymru a oedd wedi marw'r wythnos gynt: tîm Nantlle a'r Blaenau yn wynebu ei gilydd yn ddwy res dawel ysbeidiol. Hogiau o Lerpwl oedd tîm llwyddiannus y Blaenau yn y cyfnod hwnnw, ac ynghanol y tawelwch, clywyd 'sibrydiad llwydan' Orig yn torri ar y tawelwch:

"Look at these Scousers, they're shaking in their boots just looking at me."

'Roedd yn amddiffyn ei dîm oddi ar y maes hefyd, yng ngwrandawiadau bwrdd disgyblu'r Gymdeithas Bêl-droed ar 'roedd clwb Nantlle yn ymwelwyr cyson â'r Bwrdd hwnnw yn Wrecsam. Ei amddiffyniad am reg waeth nag arfer mewn ffrae rhyngddo ef ag Aled Hughes, un eiriol o ddynion garw y cyfnod, a oedd yn yr un tîm gyda llaw, oedd,

"At Nantlle we speak in the vernacular, what I said was 'Pasia'r bêl yn flippin cynt'."

The headlines said it all during my football playing career – in English and in Welsh.

The birth of a new career at the West Country boxing booths of Mickey Kiely.

A publicity shot for my new career as a wrestler.

For once, I'm airborne against my great pal Crusher Mason.

The final move before submission.

I have Eddie Hamill 'Amazing Kung Fu' secure in an arm lock.

Klondyke Bill, a great fellow traveller and part of the Bholu 'con'.

Tony St Clair.

Giant Haystacks and Pat Roach.

Steve Regal, later Lord William Regal.

The 'Amazing Kung Fu' – who later became a north Wales lifeguard.

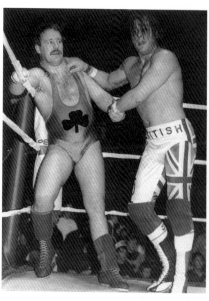

Dave 'Fit' Finlay and Tommy Bilington 'Dynamite Kid'.

Crusher Mason with my daughter Tara Bethan.

Mason Ryan (Barri Griffiths), the next Welsh superstar.

The irrepressible Adrian Street and Linda.

Antonio Inoki – one of the hardest men of all time.

The great Mitzi Mueller.

Klondyke Kate and a forced landing.

Tina Starr, who came to Rhyl as a 14-year-old. Her mother wanted me to teach her to wrestle.

Klondyke Kate – a heart of gold and a real pro.

The Mighty John Quinn.

Bholu and Akram.

The Bholu brothers – the 'sting merchants'.

Bholu, the father.

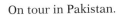
On tour in Pakistan.

The donkeys helped out to arrange the seating at our venues.

The Nigerian adventure, where the man on the throne – the Obong – controlled everything, except insects.

Reslo was a popular television series on S4C.

My days as the promoter.

At least I achieved something with Wendy's help. I am a dad and Tara is my daughter.

The 'flip-flop' National Eisteddfod 'bard'.

I was known in the Gorsedd of bards as Orig *Pehalwan*.

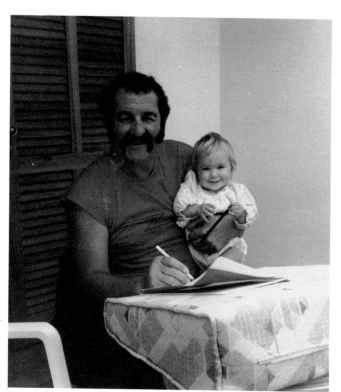

Scribbling for the *Daily Post* with my editorial assistant Tara.

Wendy and yours truly – we had a ball!

Me, Tara and Wendy.

Tara performing on stage.

Home Sweet Home. The old farmhouse (then and now) which Mighty John Quinn discovered – it's the Bandito homestead in Llansannan.

drop kicks, and so I had a suspicion that he had not seen such a ploy. Bholu smiled. He told me that he would not have loaned me the side-stake money unless he'd been confident of my victory. Had he read my fight plan? I suspect so. He was a reader of men and situations. I suspected that few had outfoxed Bholu. If they had, they would have certainly paid for it tenfold.

A man arrived from Lyallpur, now Faisalabad, and met Bholu, myself and Klondyke in our hotel at Karachi airport. He begged us to take our entourage to Faisalabad to put on a show there against the local wrestlers. We left the negotiations to Bholu. They lasted for two days. Never without his solicitor and interpreter, Bholu was methodical, and I often thought that the negotiation of the deal was far more appealing to him than the execution of it. The end result was that we would have two nights of wrestling against the local champions. Our man from Faisalabad claimed that his wrestlers were of high quality and eager to test their skills against us. The local promoters would keep the revenue for the first night, and we would receive the gate money on the second night, a Saturday. That was the deal, and it sounded good.

Our hosts certainly knew about marketing. On arrival, there were posters everywhere, with ten-foot-tall plastic models of the visiting wrestlers on the main square. It was carnival time, and the wrestling was the centre of attention. The hype was excellent, and demand was high. Once again, the venue was a test cricket ground with a capacity of 80,000 – the cricket grounds left by the British were being put to good use. The fights were scheduled to begin at six o'clock, but delays were inevitable in this part of the world, and we were quite used to them. Promoters would wait until the very last punter had paid before commencing. On the first night, a two-hour delay became three hours – we could not understand why. The gates had not been opened and there were more than 80,000 impatient punters outside. We came across a heated discussion, with Akram at the centre of attention, surrounded by the boisterous, yet nervous looking local promoters. Akram had changed his mind. He wanted the takings of the first night, and not the Saturday night. This was an extraordinary turnaround, quite beyond us and the local promoters. We kept quiet as he explained his rationale. He had seen the local fighters and had been mighty impressed. They were more than a match for his troupe, and a victorious night for the local men would more than double the gate for the Saturday show – which they could keep – if he, Akram, had the first night take. It was a most generous offer, he explained. The offer was accepted. The gates were opened and the thousands poured in for a show that was now more than three hours late. What was to follow was something of a local travesty.

Klondyke won his match with ease. Akram made short shrift of his opponent. The silence was altogether too eerie. The crowd could not believe what was going on. Their local champions were being demolished and the silence was deafening. Soon, it was my turn against the local champion Mazar Hassan-Dar. Again, strength was his forte; experience was mine.

One of the first principles in wrestling is to try and get behind your man. No matter how strong the opponent, there is little he can do to overcome you if his back is turned. Since most of my opponents were larger and stronger, it was a technique that I had learned very quickly. This particular night was no exception. I turned him around and kept him there for five rounds. By then it was all over.

It was all over for the crowd as well. They had been promised a wonderful victorious night. A night to applaud their champions over the visiting foreigners was not to be. The PA announcer proclaimed that in two days' time there would be another extravaganza of wrestling, where the local boys would seek revenge. He implored them to pray to Allah to give the defeated stars strength, and to right the wrongs they had just witnessed. Judging by the silent departing shuffle of 80,000 pairs of feet, they seemed less than convinced that their men were up to it.

Six o'clock in the morning, after a solid sleep, I was woken up by a smiling Bholu. He had a finger pressed against his lips and whispered "Karachi" to Klon and myself. He picked up our bags and pointed towards the door. It dawned on me that this was a 'planned' early departure, and that there wasn't going to be another night in Faisalabad. We went downstairs and climbed aboard an awaiting minibus. The Bholus and Akram were already inside, sitting in the front seats, alongside the minibus driver. Between them was a very large sack. Our journey continued until we arrived at a road-side café. Breakfast, with the bag in tow, was the customary six eggs fried in dead-insect-floating oil. When it came time to pay, Bholu, just like the Buckingham Palace family, had no money on him. Akram opened the bag and pulled out a 100 rupee note. I suspected by now what was in this precious bag, which had not left Akram or the Bholus' sight since departing from the hotel. I was also aware that we were in the middle of nowhere. What if we were stopped? What about the promoters in Faisalabad? Would they come after us?

We were heading for Lahore airport. We missed the first plane, and the second flight was already boarding and was fully booked. Bholu went to look for the airline's chief executive. What transpired during that conversation, and what transaction was made, I can only guess. Six passengers, already comfortable in their seats were ejected, and the chief executive loaded our luggage. Unfortunately, he also picked up the bag. Akram jumped over the counter to retrieve it. It was the only time I can recall seeing Bholu panic!

Once aboard, and Lahore bound, curiosity compelled me to ask what was in the bag.

"Are last night's takings in that bag?" I asked. Once again, he placed his finger on his lips and smiled. Enough said! "I have never seen a sack like that full of money," I told him. "When we arrive in Karachi, I would appreciate having a look." This was no coal sack sized bag; this was the size used by the farmers of Ysbyty Ifan to collect wool! Bholu smiled again and nodded. He was as good as his word. The bag was dragged into our hotel bedroom. It was an unforgettable sight – thousands and thousands of notes. I had never seen anything like it. "Tell me, Bholu," I asked, still in a state of shock after seeing such wealth.

"Why the decision to escape when you had promised an additional night?" He said that he and the crowd knew that the local fighters had no realistic chance of winning any of the bouts and so there would not be a returning crowd on the Saturday.

83

Therefore, in order to avoid trouble when no one turned up, it was best to leave.

I suspect Bholu knew this when the first approach was made in Karachi. He reached into the bag and gave me a large handful of notes. He did the same with Klon, and then he left. Klon received £748. My share was £803. He didn't bother to count the remaining notes. It might have been a good pay day for him. For us, it was a small fortune. For Bholu, in any other part of the world, it could have been jail. But this was his part of the world – and he ran it! Here was a man who could have passengers ejected from planes because the brothers wanted seats. Not a day had gone by without him inviting us to the Lahore diamond market, which made me suspect that he had huge interests there as well.

I enjoyed returning to Pakistan a few times, but could well have been killed during one of those visits. Jamaica Kid, George Burgess, was with me. Don't ask where. I think it might have been Pir Makki, but it was certainly isolated and not a major city. I was to fight Jhara, son of Aslam Bholu, and nephew of Akram. Now Jhara was arguably the country's best wrestler at the time, much revered, and certainly attracting more attention than the country's politicians.

When we arrived at the venue, which was a concrete stadium with a floor of cinders, we soon discovered that there were no changing rooms. But, hey, this was not the first time that this had happened, so we started to strip off and get ready underneath the ring. Then, the MC on the microphone made an announcement. Jhara had been involved in a car accident and would not be able to fight. The crowd were silent, dumbfounded, because the fight between their champion and a white Brit had been the talk of the region. We were in our wrestling gear and ready, but suddenly I was aware that the crowd was getting more restless by the minute and a few cinder blocks and stones were being thrown at the ring flaps. I turned to George, "Let's get out of here now! This is going to get worse."

We gathered our clothes and made a dash for it. By this time we were being pelted by a shower of stones and anything else to hand. We were running for our lives – there was no doubt about that – and I couldn't see any hiding place. And the mob was getting larger *and* closer. On the Pakistan roadsides, you will often find steel beds with sprung mattresses, and I quickly found one. (They are used by people who have no beds of their own.) I told George, "Keep it above your head! Protect yourself from the stones!" We ran as fast as we could but they were still getting closer. We dragged this bed along the street, using it as a shield, until we thankfully saw a shop entrance. We ran inside and, with the mob chanting outside, I tried as best I could to block the doorway with the mattress. It didn't fit and try as I might, I couldn't block the doorway. We had to hold on to the mattress as much as we could. We couldn't let go, because the entire mob were now outside. The shopkeeper was exceptionally kind and allowed us to stay inside until the crowd disappeared. That took five terrifying hours. When we thought the coast was clear, we thanked the shopkeeper for his hospitality and went outside. Then, we discovered why the mattress wouldn't block the doorway. There was a goat tied to the bed! From then on, in the wrestling world, it was a common joke to check whether hotel beds had goats tied to them! It was not, I hasten to add, funny at the time.

A few years later, Akram phoned from Pakistan to announce that he was bringing the brothers to Britain and he asked whether I would handle a tour. Having seen what he could do to his countrymen, I was not at all enthusiastic and declined. Bholu could deliver massive audiences in Pakistan, but he was unlikely to draw a crowd in the UK. How wrong could I be? He arranged a number of show venues in Bradford, Liverpool, Glasgow, Leicester, Manchester and the Empire Pool in Wembley. Out of curiosity, I went along to Bradford's Park Avenue and was staggered. The stadium was full, but very few white faces could be seen. Whereas I was charging people ten shillings for my shows, Bholu was selling tickets at £5, with ringside seats at £10. Bholu, after dismissing his opponent in the first fight, stood in the middle of the ring, with a microphone in one hand and a long woolsack needle in the other. He turned to the thousands present and told them that he was raising money for an orphanage in Lahore and that he expected everyone in the stadium to contribute by placing a paper note onto the woolsack needle. The needle was sent around the crowd several times as the rest of the Bholus collected piles of notes. He repeated this act and appeal at every venue, and every venue was filled to capacity. Did I regret refusing Bholu's offer to manage the tour? Of course I did! He must have made a fortune. Although I have never heard of any orphanage being built by the Bholu money. He was the most corrupt man I have ever known.

Klondyke Bill wrestled for many years – we became lifelong friends. Unfortunately, he had to give up the game because of ill-health. He came to work for me in Rhyl as a rent-collector. His heart gave up, and he died in my service. Bholu's popularity and reign as a wrestling champion came to an end in the mid-1970s.

In a martial-arts fight publicised worldwide, the greatest of boxers, Mohammed Ali, fought against the Japanese wrestling superstar Antonio Inoki. This was televised all over the world, and Inoki, one of the most talented wrestlers ever, was deemed to be the supreme world champion. It was a sad end to the amazing career of Ali, but Inoki's presence and publicity irritated the Bholu brothers, and they demanded that Akram should challenge him. It was a mismatch. Akram was by now almost fifty years of age, whereas Inoki was thirty-three and at the height of his powers. It took place in Karachi, in front of 60,000 spectators. Inoki was far too strong, and placed Akram into a submission hold where he broke his arm. The 'Lion of Pakistan' was defeated, and I held Inoki's arm aloft as the winner, because I was the referee. Akram's reign was over, and he became very depressed. He died a few years later and a ticket was left at Heathrow, sent by the Bholus, for me to attend his funeral. Unfortunately I could not go.

CHAPTER 7

The trouble I had with women wrestlers!

THERE IS POLITICAL CORRECTNESS and Welsh Methodist correctness. I have managed to ignore both with astonishing success. The former is turning us into a moronic state of obedience to values and habits that would be totally alien to generations in the past. 'Huns' were Germans, 'Frogs' were French, 'Micks' were Irish and 'Taffs' were Welsh.

What would the 'ethnic' brigade have made of us travelling wrestlers – Red Indians, black Africans, Muslim grapplers and Irish ruffians? We called ourselves the most despicable of earthy names in rings, cars, hotels and planes – but we got on in life – because we were survivors. I cannot recall any term of affection or respect coming from the lips of my great friend Giant Haystacks. It would have been deemed a failing.

I remember the collections of money for missionary work in the local chapel – pennies that were given to some destitute African village, destined to become indoctrinated by Christian virtues and habits. What a load of corrective bull! Try living successfully on the road with a van-load of smelly, pill-taking, argumentative monsters with questionable backgrounds – it would test anyone's 'faith' in mankind.

I have been called a 'Welsh bastard' on most continents, but it has never occurred to me that I should protest to some 'do-good civil rights' board' run by concerned pen pushers who can't find a worthwhile profession. I was always a committed and convicted 'Welsh bastard' – and Methodist. But the Welsh Methodist correctness is far more sinister. It is a world of whispers, hypocrisy, twitching lace curtains, scowls, rumours and merciless character assassinations. I know, because I became a victim. "How could you?" "What on earth are you doing?" These were the polite questions. Behind my back, however, I am sure that I was being boiled in oil, my birthright questioned and sent well beyond Coventry. I was also totally convinced that my relatives in Ysbyty Ifan and Abersoch would not approve either. That is why I worked on the Isle of Man for a few years and then decided I'd move to either Blackpool or Rhyl where there were more people like me – that is, bandits and crooks!

And my crime? I introduced women wrestlers! Up and down the country, barricades were set up, council officers refused to see me, the owners of halls suddenly became unavailable and the tabloids had a field day! There was always one self-opinionated, hat-pinned, Harris tweed female councillor who would object to women wrestling in her town or parish. They would spout their indignation, since such utterances would attract publicity, fame and cement her in a bucket of WI goodwill. Inevitably – and I do not know how – they would have their mayors and chief executives in their purses and pockets too. "It is degrading", they would argue and we would have hell of a fight to stage a show. Even that journalistic pillar of morality, the *News of the World*, had a go at us with condemning headlines! Tomorrow's fish and chip paper.

It began with Chunky Hayes, an independent wrestling promoter in Manchester. Chunky was not a member of the 'Big Six' wrestling circle and, in order to survive, Chunky would come up with all manner of gimmicks. In truth, his stable of wrestlers would have done well to grace a horror show. He had teenage boys fight grandparents or ageing wrestlers who should have long retired. No doubt it was a struggle for Chunky, but he did introduce women wrestlers to the UK. And what a success it became. He had already introduced Mitzi Mueller to British audiences – surely his most inspiring introduction. Mitzi became a household star, and a real hard-working pro and friend. The 'Big Six' became aware of the crowds that Chunky was pulling. Here was a market that had up until then been rejected. Female wrestlers were already accepted in the US and elsewhere, but would they become popular in the UK?

Chunky was struggling with the political backlash against women wrestlers, and as a one-man-outfit he didn't have the resources for a fair scrap with the media. So the 'Big Six' stepped in, including myself, and recruited his female entourage. We were convinced that Chunky had stumbled onto a good thing! The negative headlines were a marketing godsend. It was degrading, unladylike, demeaning, outrageous and disgusting. Bloody marvellous copy!

I must admit that when I first introduced the girls, I wasn't quite prepared myself for the protesting turbulence. I was also conscious that my Bible-reading relatives would somehow hear of this, but I had already been condemned in those quarters anyway. The press were onto us from day one. This was not necessarily a bad thing, though the daily negative headlines were a fabricated and hypocritical distraction. They milked the story, and the more column inches and photographs published, the less I had to spend on marketing. The fans were curious to see the novelty of female wrestling, and the 'bad' publicity was better than hours of distributing flyers. And what is more, those who wrote the condemning articles always wanted free tickets!

But councils and councillors – being what they were, hypocritical closet deacons – were always against us, especially in Wales and, as soon as we placed a poster anywhere, which was just about everywhere, the fire and damnation tirades began. Clerks would ring and humbly apologise, probably being monitored by listening peers, and mumble that due to public opinion we could not go ahead with our show – and we would have to cancel. I learned quickly to book halls without being specific as to the people involved. In most cases, I would pay the full hiring fee and have the contract countersigned. We would leave it until the last minute before advertising our women wrestlers, since we knew most councillors would not have any idea of what was being held in their precious halls. They would turn up for the local flower or horticultural show, or even the local scout group, especially if there was a press photographer about. When the news got out that there were women wrestlers on the bill, it would create pandemonium in the mayor's chambers. So, threatened with cancellation, a message inevitably delivered by some bespectacled minion from an admin department, we would put into action Plan B.

I would ring back, speak to the clerk and tell him, in no uncertain manner, that with a contract in hand, I had the best press contacts in the land and they would love a story about a council wanting to ban an event which was going to be a sell out. I would mention the *Daily Mirror* or *Daily Express* in passing and the fear of being highlighted in a national daily would usually do the trick. In fact, it was a ploy to generate even more publicity for a 'disgraceful event'. Sometimes, those mayoral chains should have been put to better use!

But, I had my 'ladies'. Handling men and villains was a picnic compared with my ladies. My first ones were Naughty Nancy Barton and Mitzi Mueller, both from Manchester. Super girls and super companions. Then, I was approached by a mother who told me that her daughter had no academic future, so could I possibly teach her how to wrestle? She was fourteen-years-old, and it is strange how many of the girls started at that age. That is how I began training young Tina Tate, who was a most willing pupil, and was destined to become a star on both sides of the Atlantic under the name Tina Starr.

I came across another protégé purely by accident. I was driving through Llandudno late at night having returned from a show. Outside Marks and Spencer there was an enormous fight going on, typical of the town after last orders. This was serious enjoyable stuff for any promoter. Late night fights were always a good breeding ground for would-be wrestlers. And here was one fit young lady handing out some severe punishment on a Llandudno street-corner. Her fists and legs were flying everywhere and she had no fear. Then, the police arrived, spoiling what was a pretty good fight, and the young girl was carted away. I made a point of being in court when she appeared before the town's magistrates. Before her court appearance I had also established where she worked and had met her. I had the means of finding out anything in Llandudno and Rhyl.

Her name was Bella Ogunlana, and she was employed at the

nearby Grand Hotel. I explained who I was, and why I had been very impressed by her fighting spirit. However, she was far more concerned at what would happen to her in court, how she would pay the inevitable fine and what her family would think about her behaviour. Naturally, I took advantage of the situation, assuring her that I would pay any fine providing she would come and be trained as a wrestler, and she could repay the court costs out of her winnings. What a charitable soul!

The fight had started with someone calling her a 'black panther'. What a wonderful name for a wrestling poster – and that is who she became. She was also one of the ablest of wrestlers to enter my so-called garage academy. Her family lived in Nigeria, and I remembered being told that Nigeria was ripe for wrestling promotions since it was considered then to be one of Africa's wealthiest nations. I had a contact called Power Mike, and I lost no time in contacting him to relate the news that I had found a potential national Nigerian champion.

Power Mike was an immense wheeler-dealer and well connected to a fearsome tribe. He feared no one and when contact was made, he made a counter offer at once. What about a Women's World Wrestling Championship in Lagos? Not just one female – newly discovered in a Llandudno street fight – but a championship featuring the top names in the game. And money was no barrier! He would pay for the flights and the hotels. Can you imagine the excitement, the challenge? There was one slight problem, where was I going to find these girls?

But this was a once in a lifetime opportunity – and the telephone bills over the next few weeks were the equivalent of a lifetime savings' account. There were calls to the United States, Japan, Europe, Scandinavia and any place that had staged female wrestling. Soon I was able to phone Power Mike with the news that the girls were coming! And what a line up: I had twenty-four of them. Top names like Princess Jasmine from Chicago, Beverly Shade from Florida, Natasha from South Carolina, Debbie from Tennessee, Lola Gracia and Conchita Suarez from Italy, Mimmi from Japan, Rusty Blair from Scotland, and my own Bella from Llandudno.

Having employed and toured with the likes of Klondyke Bill, Chief Thunderbird, Giant Haystacks and even employed Big Daddy, nothing could have prepared me for being the male matron to a female wrestling entourage. They complained and bitched from dawn till dusk. Nothing was right. Everything was wrong. Power Mike was not only wealthy, but was also something of a psychologist. He had foreseen that having twenty-four backstabbing, opinionated females might cause friction. So, it was heartening to hear that he'd booked eight different hotels to accommodate them. The strategy had limited success.

The Women's Wrestling World Championship was an outstanding event, though my primary role in getting twenty-four females to the stadium on time (and on the same date) was an exacting one. Lagos traffic, even in those days, presented a logistical problem. But the Nigerians turned up in their thousands, a far cry from the anti-female wrestling protests I had to endure in the market halls of Wales. What was particularly pleasing was that my Bella from Llandudno won the title, defeating Princess Jasmine in the final. Yes, she was from Nigeria, she was mine and she had met a shed-load of relatives during our stay there, so certainly, she was a popular winner! She returned to Wales and sadly never visited Nigeria again, and after another six months gave up wrestling to become a conveyor-belt factory worker in north Wales. She could have become a superstar. But Nigeria had been a new market for me, and with Power Mike as a willing accomplice, this was a new horizon. I didn't particularly care for the country, as it had its troubles even then, but I returned several times more.

At home, my female wrestlers continued to attract great crowds and protesting headlines. We were banned by local authorities, chucked out by a hall owner in Northern Ireland (who claimed that they were too scantily dressed), but Mitzi, Nancy, Rusty and Klondyke Kate and Viv Martell were becoming household names, and deservedly so. I worked out a plan to counter the opposition. I had thousands of posters made, with a blank space at the bottom. We would go around the shops and pubs with these posters and then return to fill in the blank space a few days before the show. That would do the trick, and it didn't give the enemy much time to respond. Outside the halls, with about half an hour to show time, we would have huge queues. All were ticketless, so I would send one of the wrestlers up and down the pavements shouting, "Tickets only! Tickets only! Show your tickets please!" Then, with about ten minutes to go, the same wrestler would work the crowd again, "Standing room only – Standing room only, £10 a ticket." £10 was our top price, but now there would be a panic. The halls would be packed with standing customers, all having paid £10. Halcyon days!

It was during this period that I realised the importance of looking after caretakers. Yes, the ones who shuffled around, complaining about everything, especially their employers – the council. They were at the bottom of the pay structure and did not like any evening work if it could be avoided. Since we would frequently use the same venues, you would get to know these characters. Some would regard you as a bloody nuisance and would stand around telling you what you could or could not do – always with a miserable face and a bent body which would rather be on a sofa at home watching *Coronation Street*. But the others were far more accommodating, especially if they sniffed that there might be a bung in the offing.

Most of these halls had a set number of seats once we'd erected the ring. But there was often more space available, at the back or on the sides, which could be used for standing spectators. It might cost me from £5 to £40 to buy off a caretaker, for him to turn a blind eye to what was going on, but it was worth it. By having standing-room only spaces for late punters, we could, in some places, double the audience. If a hall had been designed to hold 600 people, it naturally made a huge difference if we squeezed 1,200 in. We'd keep standing only spectators waiting as long as possible, since there is nothing like a queue to arouse interest and curiosity. When the women wrestlers were in town, every 'caretaker' investment reaped huge dividends. It was the same everywhere, Scotland, Wales, Northern Ireland and England. I had a short list of friendly, bendable caretakers. It was different in Ireland, because the priests were in charge of the halls, and they were worldly wise professionals.

If there was one individual who embraced the game, it was KK – Klondyke Kate. She became the best female 'villain' in the business. She began her career in challenge fights in Blackpool with Bobby Barron, but when I saw her first, I wasn't that impressed. "I've heard about you," she said to me in Blackpool. "You're Orig, and I hear you're a nasty bastard! But I want to be a wrestler."

"Huh," I replied, "and you are nothing more than a fast bastard. You'll never make a wrestler as long as you've got a hole in your arse." Not bad for first introductions, but it was the start of a lifelong friendship. I don't think I ever came across anyone so determined to make the grade. Kate was gutsy from the beginning, a perfect villain with a heart of gold. She would put up with anything. She was a hefty soul, with a huge personality, and a hunger for learning the trade. When she came to the Rhyl garage to train with Crusher Mason and myself, she left battered and bruised every day – but determined to make it.

She was so intent that she was game for anything. The women wrestlers were still controversial and still attracting opposition. I recall one Irish priest refusing us the use of a hall if we had women wrestlers on the show. I had only taken six wrestlers on that trip, and that included Klondyke Kate and Tina Starr. There was nothing else I could do but ask both of them to fight dressed as men. Now anyone who has seen Kate over the years will realise what a challenge that presented. But off she went to be taped up in the appropriate places, including a sock in front of her knickers. I didn't believe it was possible, since Kate was heavily blessed in all directions – especially the bust. It did the trick, but as her fight with Peter Nulty progressed, the tapes began to loosen under the strain. It was a case of having to call for a quick submission and retreat. The priest, the cause of this debacle, knew what we were up to and probably laughed all the way to his altar.

Then, along came a major break from an unexpected quarter – right in my own backyard. It came with the introduction of the

Welsh-language channel S4C in 1982. There had been a growing demand, both politically and culturally, for the establishment of a Welsh-language television channel. It was argued, quite correctly, that the language was losing ground in numbers and usage, due partly to the predominant position of the English-language media in Wales. Gwynfor Evans, the president of Plaid Cymru had championed the cause by threatening to go on hunger strike if the TV channel was not established. The government eventually relented, and the public was asked what sort of programmes they would like to see on the new TV channel.

I was not slow in responding, and with a mushrooming of small independent television production companies, I was able persuade S4C to feature wrestling on a weekly basis. This was a golden opportunity. Greg Dyke, the head of ITV, had already pulled the plug on Saturday afternoon wrestling. Joint Promotions, or rather Max Crabtree, had lost his platform stage and biggest promotional tool. The likes of Mick McManus, Jackie Pallo were no longer seen on a weekly basis and attendances were dwindling. Pallo left, as did many others, leaving Crabtree to rely on the pulling power of Big Daddy (Shirley Crabtree) and his brother Brian. It was the beginning of the end for Joint Promotions and guess who had the only TV show in town? Even Big Daddy and Pallo wrestled for me on *Reslo* – since that was the imaginative Welsh name for our weekly wrestling show. We toured around the halls and leisure centres of Wales and then I approached S4C with the idea of introducing women wrestlers.

I am still not sure whether the TV executives were aware of the fierce opposition to seeing females in the ring, because permission was granted without fuss or debate. It wasn't the first time I would wonder whether these TV types knew what was going on in the real world. The new channel needed viewers – and we did our bit. It attracted a few sniping editorials, and of course they were most welcome. Nothing like a piece of condemned entertainment to produce queues!

I also knew it wouldn't go down very well in the chapels of Abersoch and Llŷn, but it did elsewhere, and as most of the viewers were not Welsh speaking, the impact on our road show audiences was spectacular. It also helped that S4C was also transmitted in Ireland, which was already a well-trodden destination.

I was now being inundated by the country's best-known wrestlers, including those who had shunned us before! Our fees were better, there was some exposure and the gimmick of Big Daddy had run its course. And as for Pallo – we never did get on. He was a self-opinionated character, comfortable only in his own company. He did himself no favours by writing a book and exposing us all to ridicule. There is no question that in the ring he was a first-class operator – but the book *I'll Grunt, and You'll Groan* made him look like a first-class prat! But I would have to concede that if he was on your bill, then you'd have a full-house.

We toured the length and breadth of Britain and Ireland. It was nothing for our wrestlers, and those of other promoters, to fight in south-west England on a Monday night, travel to the Midlands or Lancashire mid-week, and end up in front of those fierce audiences in Scotland by the Friday night. And no one refused the Irish trips – male or female! These were good days, and if there was ever an Irish trip in the making, Giant Haystacks was on it! But, you did not dare let him drive since he was prone to fall asleep. If I wanted to make him shut up and sleep, the recitation of poems by Welsh bards would always do the trick! Haystacks listened to volumes of Welsh cynghanedd (strict-metre poetry) written by Cynan, T H Parry-Williams and Gwenallt, in particular. All six foot eleven inches and forty-five stone of him pole-axed by poetry! But Haystacks was always delighted to come to Wales. It had a ferry to Ireland, the S4C transmissions were seen in Ireland, there was plenty of work and he could call me a 'Welsh bastard' all day.

CHAPTER 8

Mother Ireland

Turpin and 'Haystacks'

SHOULD THE IRISH ECONOMY ever have to face insolvency, I would hand all financial matters over to the clergy of the Catholic Church. The Fathers and priests of the Irish Catholic Church are the most hard-nosed, manipulative bunch of entrepreneurs I have ever come across – and that is praise indeed from someone who has been in a few tight spots. That is not to say they are dishonest – but devious and imaginative resourceful rogues, yes!

I have spent the best part of thirty years travelling Ireland and putting on wrestling shows. It has always been a land I have admired and, in truth, if I hadn't been born Welsh, being born Irish would have pleased me immensely. There was no greater pleasure than driving along those challenging roads with the car windows open, listening to the rebel songs. I'd often book a venue because I liked the song – Athenry, and Ballyjamesduff to name but two of a few hundred I would sing.

In the rural areas, where life had been rough and tough, the wrestling shows appealed greatly. There is nothing like a wrestling show in Ireland. It is the land of the 'red scarf' man, but more of that later. This is also the land of hard-drinking tinkers, bare-knuckle fighting and horse racing on open roads. I have always been comfortable in the company of the Irish. When we first put on shows in Ireland, we wouldn't have advanced ticket sales. It was simpler to have everyone pay at the door. Normally we would start our shows at eight, but the Irish are notoriously bad timekeepers – I don't know why some of them wear watches.

Once, we were in Cardonagh, County Donegal, and had a good-sized hall booked. Unfortunately at eight o'clock, there was nobody inside. We waited, but there was not a soul to be seen. By 8.30, now facing a total wipe-out of an evening, we contemplated cancellation and called the hall's owner. He didn't seem concerned at all, but offered to buy the show from us. At least we wouldn't go away empty handed and some of our costs would be covered. I agreed. Fifteen minutes later, the hall was full to the rafters, with 600 people inside it. I had been well and truly cooked, and never 'sold' a show again. The simple message was, 'don't advertise a start time in Ireland, they will tell you when it's convenient for them to turn up!'

But this is also where my problems started, with the Catholic Church 'entrepreneurs'. The rural areas had small church halls, and that was always going to be a challenge. The capacity of most of them was extremely limited, and invariably they had low ceilings. No good for wrestling, no good at all! By the time we would have erected a ring in some of the halls, there'd only be space for a priest and his friends. But the Irish do not believe in problems – only solutions. "How tall is the ceiling of your hall?" I would ask.

"How tall do you want it?" would be the reply.

I was extremely naive when we started the Irish tours. They were organised from our Rhyl base in north Wales. Arrangements were made by phone to Ireland. Inevitably, the only man with a hall in the town would be the local priest! And were they all really called Father Murphy? "Sure we've got a hall – and a grand hall it is too," was the usual response. Terms were negotiated, the date was booked, tickets and posters sent. The problem with this arrangement was that I didn't know who was on the other end of the phone. My! I've met some real operators in collars.

We would plan some thirty shows on the road. Initially we would stick to the north and east, as that is where people watched the wrestling on ITV, so some of our fighters were known to them already. Later, as Sky TV's WWF and WWE shows became popular, we could go just about anywhere. The Irish tours were popular with the wrestlers as well. True, in the initial stages we were limited in budget and travelling facilities, but that improved with not everyone having to travel in the 'ring van' any more.

You can just imagine our horror on arrival to find a hall that could barely stage a whist drive, let alone a wrestling show. Giant Haystacks? He could head-butt the lights!

"We can't wrestle here. It's too small," I would protest. Then the banter and barter would start. "Well Mr Williams, I am not sure what can be done. There are hundreds coming along for the show tonight, and there will be a riot if they can't get in. It's been the talk around here for some time now. I don't know what we can do for you."

It was always the same. And of course the small little question of the deposit, which had already been sent, was never mentioned. "I'll tell you what we can do." Oh! How I came to love that phrase, since I knew what was coming.

"My cousin lives some fifteen miles away. Now, his village has a hall four times the size of ours, the biggest hall in the whole of Ireland, and he is very friendly with the Father who looks after it. That one would do you fine. I'll make the arrangements." And before you could respond about the logistics of erecting the ring, he was off to find his cousin (if he existed) and the Father – both of them probably parked around the corner.

Having already forfeited the original money, I would end up paying the priest and the cousin would expect a back hander as well. It was the way of Ireland. All of this would have been planned by my Irish friends before we arrived, since there was never a sight of the posters which had been sent. We would then find them plastered all over the alternative venue, neatly changed or altered, but showing that they were well-weathered.

There was one incident I recall vividly. We had arrived in a small village in Donegal. The village might have been small, but the hall was colossal. This booking, made by Paddy Jennings, a local shopkeeper, had troubled me since I'd not heard from him for weeks. As soon as we arrived I went looking for Mr Jennings. "How are the tickets going?" I asked.

"Wonderfully well! They have all gone. The whole lot! You'll have a fine turnout," said Paddy, without making eye contact. This was very encouraging as we would expect money up front to pay the lads. Naturally, the next question was about the money. "I have no money," he said, "I gave the tickets away." The Welsh expletives pierced the Irish mist!

Then he proceeded. "Cool down man, and listen to what I have done. You sent me one thousand tickets, but the hall will take three thousand people. So I sent tickets to all the neighbouring villages, and they all want to come. So that is one ticket for the driver and he will have three passengers – and they will pay!" I quickly calculated that this man, Paddy Jennings, was a financial genius, and then he told me that the Father would want free entry, with a few of his friends. We were truly blessed that night in Donegal. They came in droves.

It was a steep educational process. Late changes of venue happened frequently. There was one occasion when our ring collapsed because the building wasn't strong enough to hold the support ropes. And we were only a couple of hours away from show time. No problem at all! A change of venue, and a priest's call to the local Gaelic radio station, providing he and his family (all seventeen of them) could enter for nothing. It was done, seemingly, on the spur of the moment. Or was it calculated chaos? That night, to my sheer astonishment, only one car turned up at the old venue and we had a packed house at the alternative hall. Crisis? What crisis? Call for a priest!

I quickly accepted – or had to accept – that whatever the situation, they usually had you by the short 'n' curlies! Some would say that the advance tickets had never arrived, or didn't even know the show had been booked. Then, they would offer all manner of assistance, providing they could have share of the gate and a cluster of free passes. The strange thing was that these were often our better attended shows.

I'd settled on a £450 fee for the hire of a village hall with a certain Father Murphy. When we arrived there was no sign of him at the appointed time, and so we were sent down the road only to find our friend on top of a ladder painting his house. He knew exactly who we were but asked, "Would you be the wrestling people?" Once acknowledged, he told me that he had some bad news. "I've given you the hall far too cheaply!"

"Here we go," I said to myself.

"The hall will be packed out this evening – some three thousand people – so you can have it for £1,000. If you don't take the offer – there will be a riot!" He even offered a smile as he said it. This, from a man who baptised, blessed and buried in God's name! I knew I was being cooked by the cleric, but a compromise was reached. There would be a £2 surcharge at the gate – and the Father himself would announce it to the queues outside. There is no way that I could have done that without being lynched, but he got away with it, and I suspect he allowed a few hundred more inside as long as they parted with two punts.

Of the hundreds of wrestlers who have travelled with me to Ireland, two deserve special mention here. When I decided to give up life on the booths and go it on my own as a promoter, I knew that I had to have a 'name' to pull in the crowds. Wrestling was big business and drawing huge crowds due to its success on Saturday afternoon TV. All the big names were signed up by Joint Promotions, a cartel of six independent promoters, and this was the beginning of my war with them over the next thirty years. They had made Jackie Pallo, Mick McManus, Big Daddy and many others household names. I had constantly tried to be ahead of the game, and luck was on my side right from the beginning.

My very first signing for an Irish tour was Randolph Turpin. He had already won and lost the boxing middleweight championship of the world against Sugar Ray Robinson. Randolph was the hardest hitting boxer I had seen, but he was no businessman, and I have little doubt that he lost his return title fight in New York due to outside influences – undoubtedly his chosen lifestyle with the opposite sex. He told me tales of the Mafia threats if he had won the return fight. However, I suspect that it was the partying and the girls, which never really stopped, that was to blame.

Before setting off for the United States, he had established his training camp at Gwrych Castle, near Abergele in north Wales. He met Gwen, his second wife there, and after returning home he bought the castle and Llandudno's Great Orme as a retirement investment. The castle and the café turned out to be financial disasters, and those around him, apart from Gwen, took full advantage of his misplaced trust and generosity.

Alas, the tax man came to hunt him down as well, and Randolph suddenly went from being the golden boxing hero from Leamington Spa to being a penniless soul. His tale, after the Robinson fight, was punctuated by a few highs but generally it was a life that turned into terminal decline. There was an acrimonious divorce from his first wife, allegations of brutality and rape from an American lover and the steady loss of financial reserves to those who professed to be his friends. He just couldn't cope and he lost everything.

I met him on the Isle of Man. He appeared to be cheerful, and at that time he was still in good shape and drinking little. There was no hiding from the fact that he was still a ladies man. How else could you explain the squandering of a small fortune? He'd earned £150,000 in fifteen months – when the average weekly pay was £10! He'd been wrestling for a few months when we met, for a fair number of promoters, joining a list of illustrious boxers who had swapped gloves for holds and grapples – Primo Carnera, Jack Dempsey, Joe Louis, Jersey Joe Walcott, and of course since then, Mohammad Ali, Mike Tyson and Joe Erskine. It was a way of earning money, and though he kept boxing, his decision to wrestle was not universally welcomed. Some commentators saw it as a fall from grace. The novelty soon wore off for him as well, since the travel was not to his liking. But it was something to do. There was a ring, a crowd, lights and a fee.

Gradually a lot of the promoters lost interest in Turpin. He was absent-minded and couldn't be relied upon to turn up. His health was not good and the punishment he'd received in the ring was becoming more evident by the day. He also had to face the reality of his financial ruin. I was also in a similar situation. I'd left football, the booths and was looking for direction. I was also skint. I knew the ways of the booths and I had been taught how to promote by Mickey Kiely. My decision was made. I arranged a road show in Ireland, my first of I don't know how many. And who better to top the bill than Randolph Turpin? He was still box office and not many black sportsmen had been seen in Ireland. He immediately said yes, and I have no doubt that a trip to Ireland was a form of escapism for him also.

I planned the tour carefully. Most of Ireland didn't have a clue what professional wrestling was all about – apart from those who could, at that time, receive ITV's *World of Wrestling*. So, as already mentioned, we stuck to the north and east. When Sky TV came along much later, it was entirely different. I hit gold and I had great success in World Wrestling look-a-like shows. So for ten days we roamed these Irish halls and towns – and what a great crowd puller Turpin was! He wrestled or 'boxed' against Doctor Death and was part of a show featuring my old pal from the booths Gordon Corbett, a Red Indian Thunderbirds tag team and two wrestling midgets – 'Tiny Tim Gallagher' and 'Gorgeous' Fuzzy Kaye, who, incidentally, was well connected with the Kray twins. A motley crew to start with. There would be other characters far more bizarre.

Turpin enjoyed himself, because here was the adulation of the past, the lights, the buzz and he had company. He did his bit, and I will never forget two old Irish women walking out from one of the shows. One said to the other, "That man Turpin was really great, but the rest of it was a fierce bluff!" But, inevitably, as was often the case in the land of bare-knuckle fighting and 'red scarves', someone would want to have a go at Turpin. We became used to it and predictably it always happened in pubs towards closing time. He'd be challenged to arm wrestle the local champion. "Seamus will have you; he's not been beaten in these parts for ten years." The challenge would be accepted, providing a £20 wager was set aside, but on one condition: the challenger would have to arm wrestle Fuzzy Kaye, one of the midgets in order to qualify to take on Turpin. There'd be no problem in raising the wager in the bar. And a crowd would gather. You'll never beat a midget in an arm wrestle. Your arm is at a weakened angle from the start and your force only pushes the midget's arm into a lock. Oh, how we enjoyed collecting the money, night after night, and Randy never once arm wrestled. We had great fun.

Then on the Saturday night after our return, his wife Gwen

rang me to say that Randy had shot and killed himself. I had no idea of what torment he was going through. I suspect that he could not cope with the short-lived success he had achieved, and certainly could not cope with the financial pressures and failure, mainly caused by hangers on and, quite possibly, by the men with Inland Revenue briefcases. In his prime he was a superb physical specimen. What a tragic loss.

We would always stay in a 'cause' hotel on our travels. These were our audience, and indeed we had more affinity with them. They also gave us some security. The British Army was always in evidence in Ireland, and on more than one occasion they would disrupt our shows by marching in unannounced with guns menacingly waved in the air. "The 'Maureens' [a reference to Maureen O'Hara] are coming," would be the whisper, whether in a wrestling hall or a bar. Suddenly, the atmosphere would change as the soldiers marched in, kicking and wrecking the furniture. I was witness to brutality of the worst kind, especially against teenagers who were not much younger than the soldiers pointing guns down their throats.

"Everything all right, sergeant?" we would ask, as a teenager had an army gun in his mouth. I often felt that the British army, as I had seen it, had prolonged the troubles in Northern Ireland rather than resolved them. It was a tragic and brutal period for Ireland. Yet for one individual, travelling to Ireland was pure bliss.

His name was Martin Ruane, and he was born in Camberwell, London. But if you dared mention that fact, you could have been in danger of losing a limb. As soon as we boarded the ferry from Holyhead to Dublin, his accent would change from Cockney to Irish and he would begin his familiar routine of telling you all about his family who hailed from Kiltmagh in County Mayo. He insisted that he was born there – and few would challenge this claim, even though everyone knew better.

This was 'Giant Haystacks': friend, raconteur, pain in the backside, twenty-two carat star. Although six foot eleven inches tall (seven foot on the posters) and forty-two stone (forty-five on the posters), he could act in the most childish way one minute, and hold an intellectual discussion on an unlikely subject the next. From the moment he called me a 'Welsh bastard' I knew that this would be a troublesome lifelong friendship. I would always return the compliment with aptly chosen words. He had absorbed Irish folklore, but had an obsession for the life and times of world heavyweight champion Gene Tunney, a man with Kiltmagh connections. Haystacks claimed Tunney was born there, but the Haystack claims did not always agree with fact. Indeed, his stories were always entertaining, but they varied in content with every re-telling.

If you had an hour or two to spare, just the mere mention of Paul McCartney or Frank Sinatra would do the trick. Haystacks had met both. Sinatra had spoken to him at the Royal Albert Hall in London. The conversation could not have lasted more than a minute, but the account would take the best part of an hour. "Did I tell you I am an honorary ambassador for Zimbabwe?" he'd ask. "Yes," you'd answer, knowing full well that you were about to hear the same tale once again. "The Queen Mother watches me on telly – she told me!" And he told *me* that a thousand times too. "Have you seen my films?" he'd ask, and before you could answer he'd go through the entire scripts of *The Wild Bunch* or *Quest of Fire* though, in truth, he had only had cameo roles. But, to me, he was always a star!

I took him everywhere: India, Pakistan, Dubai, but Ireland was always his favourite destination. For one thing, it didn't involve booking two seats at the rear of an aeroplane and it meant that people would not gawk at his size. On those foreign trips involving planes, I'd receive a torrent of abuse. He hated planes and the only way I could shut him up was to tell him, "Listen here Stacks, what kind of man are you, if you can't put up with a little discomfort? If you don't want to come, stay at home! That will prove to me that you are a wimp and not a man." That would usually do the trick – to question his manhood would produce an hour or two of pensive peace.

I could name the hotels and guest-houses of Ireland that had seven-foot beds, and those with thick walls capable of housing and containing the extraordinary Haystacks cacophony of snores and snorts. And you dare not wake him unless you fancied being called a 'Welsh bastard' for the next twenty-four hours.

You can tell a man's strength by the size of his wrists. Haystacks had huge wrists, and he was genuinely a strong man. Other wrestlers would build themselves up by fair means or foul, but you could tell immediately whether they were naturally strong. Perhaps he was not mobile, but those on the circuit certainly knew Stacks's strength. And almost everywhere we went, a relative of Haystacks would be at the door, wanting a free ticket. There were times when I thought he had cousins everywhere – this man born in Camberwell. He'd then refuse to fight unless I'd oblige them with free tickets. It happened everywhere, even once when his 'cousin' was the local chief of police and there with his entire brood, with the hall already full to capacity. Haystacks knew that without him, the hall would be empty.

His knowledge of bare-knuckle fighting heroes was immense, and his obsession was to be the 'red scarf man'. Every Irish region had its red scarf man, the toughest man in the land, having won the honour of wearing the red scarf in a fight and having defeated all challengers after that. We had met a few and you dared not glance at them for too long because these men were real fighters and could stand the punishment of being severely beaten. Suffice to say, most arguments in Ireland were sorted out by fists and fights.

Even as a boy in Ysbyty Ifan, I had heard that a red scarf man had once visited neighbouring Llanrwst. He had no challengers and moved on. "I want to be the red scarf man," Haystacks would moan. "Fetch me a red scarf so that I can wear it, you Welsh bastard." This could go on for weeks. I would try reasoning with him.

"Listen Stacks, you are six foot eleven and forty-five bloody stone and even if you wear the red scarf in a pub – who the bloody hell is going to challenge you?"

"I don't care! Fetch a red scarf!"

A red scarf would be found and he was quite content to sit in a corner for hours awaiting a challenge – which never came.

He was certainly moody and broody and could become agitated at the slightest thing, but he was genuinely good company. His health deteriorated with age as his heart struggled to cope. He ended up as a debt collector. Can you imagine refusing this man if he arrived on your doorstep? Later, he was diagnosed with cancer and suddenly there were no more tales. To those who did the Irish tour – and they would have included Adrian Street, Johnny Saint, Dave 'Fit' Finlay, 'Rollerball' Rocco, Klondyke Bill, Tony St Clair, Mighty John Quinn, Klondyke Kate, Mitzi Mueller, Naughty Nancy and countless others – when we look back on it, we had a ball!

So we leave this game which is hard and cruel,
And down at the show on a ringside stool,
We'll watch the next man, just one more fool.

Randolph Turpin

CHAPTER 9

Have Ring – Will Travel

LIFE AS A PROMOTER in the 1960s and 1970s was a constant battle against the establishment. By 'establishment', I mean Joint Promotions, the promoters who had ITV Saturday afternoon wrestling television coverage sown up. They tried to squeeze us, the small promoters, out of halls, contractually and financially, and therefore away from the main crowd pulling wrestlers. Smaller promoters such as Paul Lincoln, Brian Dixon and I and a few others had to be grafters – inventive, quick thinking and resourceful – to survive. Paul, in particular, was a real thorn in their side, whereas Brian was hugely respected by the wrestlers, especially the ones learning their trade who had no time for Joint Promotions.

There were gimmicks galore, or should I say schemes, and we would have to admit that the popularity of wrestling on the television did us no harm at all. But there was no love lost between us and the Max Crabtrees and Dale Martins of the world, who were putting on shows around the country almost every night of the week. Paul 'Doctor Death' Lincoln was a particularly inventive promoter and produced his own star names – the Wild Man of Borneo being his best. Yet, wherever they, Joint Promotions, went with their big name TV wrestlers, we followed the next week, and although they tried to block us from hiring halls, I would counter this by booking a benign 'sporting event' at the same halls that they had just occupied. And then put on a wrestling match. There would be trouble if they knew in advance – and that could, and did, become physical. I have been known to collect a few GBH 'degrees' along the way.

I remember Paul Lincoln taking over the old Sophia Gardens Pavilion in Cardiff from Dale Martin, thus making his old venue in the city, the huge Drill Hall, available for hire. I jumped at it, and what a bonus that was, especially when I persuaded the former British heavyweight champion Joe Erskine, a local lad, to come and wrestle for me. He was too laid-back to be any good, but he did pull in the locals.

Naturally, Joint Promotions would tie the big names into exclusive contracts – or at least they would try to. It was guerrilla warfare at times, and in war, the truth sometimes becomes a casualty. Some of the tactics and antics I adopted to survive did land me in trouble, not only in the courts but also in the dark shady areas outside various halls.

I knew that within the Joint Promotions stable of wrestlers there was resentment towards the owners. The TV contract cheques were fat, whereas the envelopes to the boys were thin. We made it known to them the monetary figure of thousands that was being offered to the company by ITV, whilst they, the stars, were getting only hundreds of pounds. We offered them better money to come to us, though they could still appear on the Joint Promotions circuit. Ideal for us, but not so good for Joint Promotions! I can't count the times I was threatened.

The only option for us independents was to take wrestling shows out of the country, or to areas that did not really interest the big boys, such as the West Country, Wales, the north-west of England, Scotland and some areas that were not on the Ysbyty Ifan primary school atlas. In the early years, I had the wonderful services of Brian Dixon as my right-hand man – he was my announcer, rigger, promoter and referee. He was an indispensable and immense help, a top man, and I bitterly regret the break up of our relationship when he too decided to become an independent promoter and competitor, taking his wife Mitzi Mueller with him. He became a major promoter and an inventive producer. It took some time, far too long – some ten years in fact – before we became friends again. People will tell you that I was a stubborn and unforgiving man. I would probably have to plead guilty to these charges, and ask for a few others to be taken into consideration. There would be no shortage of witnesses. Brian's rationale was that we had a big enough promotional fight on our hands with Joint Promotions without squabbling amongst ourselves. He wanted to improve our presentation as well. Fair point – and he did.

While Brian was on board, we ventured to foreign lands. Places, I was told as a boy, where Christian missionaries used to be sent and were never heard of again. And I will tell you that no Joint Promotions shows would ever have ventured to where we went. They wouldn't have had the guts for it! Some might call it the 'Third' world. What utter nonsense! This is where I found the most ruthless first-class operators of all. Everything and everybody had a price and an angle – nothing was straightforward and I became a willing pupil at the feet of con-artists, embezzlers, crooks and schemers. Joint Promotions were chapel deacons compared with this lot. It is more than possible that our foreign escapades were connected and directed to entrepreneurial crooks! My territory.

Some of it was not at all amusing. Getting the ring to places on the atlas – not a map, mark you – was almost a commando-style exercise. The old wrestlers will tell you of the ringside hotel which meant that, as wrestlers, you were sleeping underneath the ring at night. But the ring logistics were their own nightmare. The venue ceilings were either too low or the halls were too wide for the suspension ropes. The wrestlers were never happy with the bounce of the canvas, but nothing was more problematic than getting the ring from point A to point B. And there was no worse nightmare than the trip from Rhyl to Naples. That is probably the first time those two places have been coupled!

I had been invited to take a show there by NATO – as entertainment for the troops. But by the time we arrived we'd had to go through a NATO exercise of our own. There were three of us in the Range Rover: myself, Wendy my wife, and Dave Stalford, general handyman, best mate and no mean wrestler. Behind, we had the well-travelled trailer. By the time we reached Dover, all was not well with the Range Rover. The engine was over-heating pulling the weight of the trailer and ring. Dave sourced the problem, rectified it and we boarded the ferry. I don't know how many of you are familiar with the Paris Périphérique. It is a colossal, multi-lane circular motorway around the French capital. It makes Birmingham's Bull Ring look like a village roundabout. It is a death-trap since everybody is hell-bent on getting to somewhere on time. If you miss your turning, you could spend the rest of the day circling Paris. It was on the Périphérique that we noticed that the trailer was not responding to the Range Rover's movements. It was swaying from one side to other. There was nothing to do but stop in the middle of that suicidal Formula One rush-hour. Calamity! I don't know where we lost it, but the four-wheeled trailer was no more; it was now a 'Fools and Horses' three-wheeled vehicle. And the Parisians kept whizzing past. We had lost a complete wheel. We drove, carefully, in a not-so-slow lane, looking for a garage. Nothing doing! Those who have broken down in France will know how unhelpful or ignorant they can be. We tried garages, scrap-yards, the rescue services – but to no avail. So, we decided that we would continue our journey through France and Italy with a three-wheeled trailer – and our ring.

Imagine the situation when we arrived at the French–Italian border. I got out of the car and sheepishly walked alongside the trailer, to disguise the fact we were missing a wheel. 'Del Boy' David Jason and his fabulously talented late wife and friend of mine, Myfanwy Talog, would have been proud of me. Except that this was not scripted, this was real. We passed the border point and headed for Naples. I was Welsh wrestling's 'Rodney'. It was the kind of journey that many a traveller has experienced. The next mile might be your last. Something or somebody is going to hold you up. You are no longer in control – that control and your destiny has now been transferred to a clapped-out trailer on three wheels. Those miles were slow towards Naples, but then we saw the rubber tyre lights. We'd been told about them. As we approached the American base, our destination, young girls paraded before the lights of burning tyres. These were young prostitutes, and 'Mafia placed'. We arrived, did our show, and thanks to the US army mechanics we had our trailer fixed. It had been a rich tapestry of an incident-packed journey.

But there were many more tales. It doesn't get any more bizarre than Steve Taylor and I sharing a ring in Sweden with

Miss Lee, an ageing stripper and her sexually aroused poodle, providing the half-time entertainment. Sweden, at that time, was in the middle of a sex revolution. Every street corner had a sex shop or a sex show. It was absolutely marvellous and I don't have to tell you that we were mightily distracted. I don't know why Rolf, our agent, had hired Miss Lee, because she was well past her prime and in the land where sexual freedom was everywhere to be seen, Miss Lee was something of an antidote. The show wasn't going well either. There was a 50 kronor challenge to anybody willing to take on the wrestlers and beat them. Quite a few tried in the first few days but word got around that we were not going to be defeated and gradually the crowds disappeared. Miss Lee was most distraught. She blamed us for not pulling in enough punters! She couldn't pull anything either. And you couldn't help but notice that she didn't wear knickers as she climbed into the ring, which was some eighteen feet up!

After weeks of seeing the same spectacle, the novelty had worn off. Then, one night, whilst climbing into the ring, Miss Lee urinated all over Dave. Not much bread was broken after that, and the damned dog was lucky to survive. I still have this memory of her, wearing only a fur stole towards the end of her act – attempting to gyrate, throwing the stole to the floor for the dog to have his fun with the fur. Then she'd walk off, completely naked, and climb down eighteen feet of steps. And no one took the blindest bit of notice, except for the odd schoolboy.

No matter how well you planned matters, something would always go wrong. At times I felt as if I was lurching from crisis to crisis. Being skint was not unusual. So when opportunities arose, I took them, often without thinking of the consequences. I don't think the term 'risk assessment' had been invented in those days. But there was one journey which, for those involved, will live long in the memory.

This was the trip to Turkey: on my personal Richter scale the most frightening of all places. Worse than Llanrwst on a Saturday night! I had read about, and was fascinated by, Turkey's 'oil wrestlers' whom, according to my information, wrestled smothered in oil. I had made contact with a few of the Turkish wrestlers during one of those endless German tournaments, but not much bread had been broken there. A man called Sadi Pekerol, a theatre administrator, approached me during a stint on the Isle of Man. Sadi was a Turk, English speaking, and a man with connections. Priceless! I told him of my ambitions and his offer to help was noted, though I thought little about it afterwards.

The man did not let me down. I received a letter from him explaining that there was much enthusiasm for welcoming a team of western wrestlers to the country of oil wrestlers. I did a little research and realised quickly that wrestling was a national sport in Turkey. The more I read, the more excited I became; this perhaps was the financial killing I had so often dreamt of. A letter was fired back by return of post.

I explained that if we were to bring the best wrestlers, we would require 50,000-capacity football stadiums, especially if what he said about Turkish wrestling popularity was true. And what if we brought women wrestlers as well? To say that I was excited about the Turkish expedition would be an understatement. However, I have to admit that I had an admirable record in cock-ups and disasters. I had never experienced niggling problems on these trips – just complete disasters! Never mind, I thought to myself. This is it, the 'big deal'. We were on our way to Turkey. Jim Moser, Kevin Connelly and myself had the onerous task of taking the ring, mats and all the gear from north Wales to Turkey by car and trailer. The rest would travel by plane.

There was one slight problem for us – the crew. The small matter of negotiating Belgium, Germany, the old Yugoslavia, Bulgaria – highways, low-ways, dirt tracks… apart from an ageing trailer, we were also totally incompetent linguistically. Jim did a clucking noise at one Bulgarian restaurant hoping for chicken and chips, and the waitress came back with a boiled egg – we were that bad. Nor did we know what awaited us. We were searched for drugs on the Turkish border, and we sighed with relief as we were signalled through. We had arrived in Turkey and were met by Sadi on the other side. My dream of a fortune was now very much alive. This was going to be my financial killing! Farewell the market halls of Wales! So long Merseyside, Lancashire, Wick in Scotland, and farewell Donegal! Orig Williams had arrived in the Mecca of wrestling! Mr Wrestler had arrived! Hmm... not quite.

The first stadium booked for us that night was not of first division standard. More Accrington Stanley than Old Trafford, with a capacity of 12,000, but since we were booked for two nights, I rationalised that the return would be OK. I kept the belief. We went to the airport to await the arrival of the wrestlers. It was evident that news of our visit had travelled far and wide. Hundreds had turned up at Istanbul airport together with a platoon of press photographers. This was good news indeed, and I was convinced that at last, my entrepreneurial gamble was about to pay major dividends. But I quickly realised that they were not there to see the western challengers to Turkish wrestling supremacy. They were there to see a female wrestler. And that is all they did see. Mitzi was the only one to arrive. The other female, Leyla, had failed to turn up at Heathrow on time and had missed the plane. She would arrive the next day. There was nothing I could do about it as Mitzi took centre stage for the photographers.

It took an eternity to get to the stadium as the roads were packed with cars and people, all of them heading in the same direction. By the time we arrived, all seats and vantage points were gone. There were 12,000 inside, 3,000 on surrounding buildings, walls and in trees, with thousands having been refused entry. If this scene was repeated at the other shows we had in Ankara and Izmir, my tills would ring. I took Sadi to one side before asking the wrestlers to parade around the ring. Since we only had one female wrestler, I suggested that he should make an announcement right at the beginning of the evening to say that the female bout would be postponed until the following night. Better to tell them now rather than later I thought, and Sadi agreed.

Suddenly there was a commotion, and a mighty roar. Everyone was on their feet, and I couldn't understand why. Sadi pointed to a bald gentleman who was the centre of attention. He was surrounded by huge crowds and was clearly an important and respected figure.

"That is Ordulu Mustafa," said Sadi, "he is the undefeated heavyweight wrestling champion of Turkey – and he is here to challenge you!"

"What do you mean, challenge me? This is a show not a bloody championship," I replied.

"Mustafa is a proud champion. He wants to see if he can beat the foreigners," said Sadi.

"Stuff Mustafa! Go and tell the crowd that we don't have two women wrestlers."

And then I thought that a fight between one of us and Mustafa might satisfy the crowd, and could be an even bigger attraction. "Hang on a minute Sadi. Tell Ordulu Mustafa that one of us will accept his challenge." By then I had figured that this man, still being lauded by the crowd, appeared to be just under six foot and about fourteen stone, and not a giant. But what I didn't know was how they fought as oil wrestlers – and what unknown tricks they had. Sadi disappeared, as the rest of us drew lots to find a challenger. How did I not know that the draw was fixed? Was I not amongst bandits and thieves? I could see that none of the other wrestlers – Jim Mozer, Eddie Hamill and the rest – fancied an unscripted bout. So it was the pride of Wales against the champion of Turkey. So much for the bond between wrestlers! Bloody cowards!

The first bouts went well, and we had a very attentive audience. Wrestling was a major sport in Turkey, with a major championship held every year involving over a thousand competitors. My opponent had held the title of heavyweight champion for three years. Our fight was after the interval, and again I asked Sadi to make the announcement about the female wrestling. "During the interval," he promised, so I focused my attention to the matter at hand. Ordulu looked more than six foot in the ring, and I could tell that this man was a real athlete: he had a honed body – not from a gym, but from sheer hard work – he was a natural athlete. The crowd were reaching fever-pitch, hooters, fireworks, bells, rattling tins – it was all deafening. The referee called us together –

and the bell went for the first round. I remember very little about that round. He was all over me one minute and I couldn't find him the next. He had the moves of an Olympic gymnast and in the hold he was exceptionally strong. I failed to make any impression at all, and I was resigned to having a severe beating. Whatever I did, he absorbed it, like dirt into a vacuum cleaner.

The second round was marginally better. I am not sure what rules were governing this fight – I suspected that it would be to the finish; there would be no gentlemanly holds for a submission. Every time he moved, the crowd were with him... they wanted blood. I had not met such an athletic opponent. But I was slowing him down – or so I thought. The third round was more comfortable, and I did think that if I could go the distance, whatever that was, there was a reasonable chance of a positive outcome. Between the third and fourth round I was aware that an announcement was made to the crowd. But Ordula was out of his corner, and ready. Again he launched himself into a series of fast moves. Then, suddenly, he was distracted. I dared not take my eyes off him, but I was aware that something was wrong. The noise of the crowd was different. Ordulu stopped in his tracks, and looked over my shoulder. I, too, turned. The stadium was on fire! There were six small separate fires. Chairs were being thrown and thousands were heading in a panic towards the exits. It was a timber-built stadium, and it was alight! It was sheer pandemonium.

As we ran for our lives, I was told that Sadi, in his infinite wisdom had, during our fight, announced to the crowd that there would be no women wrestlers that night. And the riot and fire was the result. The wrestlers made it to their bus, but the crowds tried to roll the vehicle over. They got away just in time! The next morning we were national news! Front page headlines, with pictures of the crowd fleeing for their lives. The fire brigade had done their best to control the fire, and although there was a fair amount of damage, we could still put on a show that night with female wrestlers – or so we thought. The stadium manager was not best pleased. He was furious. There would be no show that night, or any other night as long as he was the manager. The takings for that night – £50,000 – were confiscated in order to pay for the damages, and he more or less told us to leave the city. My protestations fell on deaf ears. Suddenly, no one could speak English. There was little we could do but leave and head for Ankara, the venue of the next show. But the tale of woe had not yet run its course. News of the Istanbul stadium fire reached Ankara and the stadium manager there said that we would have to cancel. This was turning out to be a major disaster. We pleaded and pleaded, and eventually we were granted a meeting with the city authorities. Everyone has a price, and it became obvious that a deal could be struck, but it would be a costly one. I was in a corner and they knew it, but a deal was done. It wasn't really a deal – this was a financial submission hold! This allowed us to spend the rest of the day phoning the media and trying to generate positive publicity to counter the negative headlines from Istanbul. It didn't work, since only a thousand people turned up for this show and the other shows on route. My dream of a financial killing had literally gone up in flames. Together with Jim Moser I also had to make that awful journey back to Wales to think about what might have been.

Strangely, Jim was also with me on another challenging expedition. I don't know why I had this zest for travel. Knowing how much I enjoyed being within my own square mile, it doesn't really make sense. But you can't make a fortune sitting in Rhyl or Llandudno. If you did, it would probably be nicked by the taxman anyway. I had a passion for characters and people who made things happen – or at least tried to. This naturally meant 'dealers' of some calling, and I would find them in the unlikeliest of places. The world is overpopulated by politically correct 'yes' men. Jim and I accepted an invitation from Power Mike to return to Nigeria, but I knew that nothing would be straightforward. Mike was the self-proclaimed 'hardest man in Africa'. He was one of life's operators and dealers, and was well connected. He provided evidence of that on our arrival, by organising an official meeting with the local ruler of Calabar, who had the title of Obong. I knew that the Calabar region was poor, underdeveloped and extremely tribal. Nigeria was a country in constant turmoil, having just gained its independence from Britain. I had no ideas about the rules of protocol, since wrestling promoters were not usually entertained by ruling monarchs, and I wasn't sure when we arrived at his palace as to how to greet him, so 'your majesty' would have to do.

When we entered his chamber I was delighted to see that the Obong was not at all threatening. He was an elderly man in his nineties, smiling, and of good humour. What he made of us I don't know, since he kept his own counsel. He bestowed the honour on us of being the first users of his brand new stadium. We were then invited to visit the arena. Off we went, delighted at not having been detained or arrested, since I never knew what stories ever pre-empted our arrival anywhere. The stadium was surrounded by deep jungle, and we were due to put on the opening show that evening. It was a large and splendid looking arena, but I could not help noticing that amidst the seating rows, there was the 'royal box' or the 'Obong box', complete with reclining chairs and sofas. Power Mike beamed with pleasure. The Obong seemed pleased: we were being honoured. What could go wrong? How often have I said that?

The first fight was due to start at seven o'clock, so there was plenty of time for us to have a power nap after our royal audience. My opponent would be the local champion, a man by the impressive name of Hercules Ayelah. Jim would be on first, and he would fight Ben Lionheart from Lagos. Suddenly, the hotel door flew open and in ran a very excitable Power Mike. For a black man, he looked a funny shade of white. "Orig! Orig! Wake up! There's no electricity, and we can't operate the turnstiles!" The man was becoming delirious.

"Come On! What can we do?" I did register that this crisis was now a collective responsibility. Power Mike was the promoter; we were mere hired assassins, who were about to become electricians.

It was indeed a crisis, since the darkened stadium was already filling up with a few thousand people sitting quietly in their seats and waiting, with only the odd flame of a cigarette lighter to tell you that they were there. Power Mike was frightened – I could see that. I suggested that he should ask everyone to turn their cars towards the turnstiles, so that the ticket takers could see what they were doing. That having been done he disappeared and we couldn't find him anywhere. With the turnstiles clicking, the stadium was already full, but still no lights. Someone suggested that it was customary not to turn outside lights on, because the insects would swarm all over them. Now that sounded a reasonable explanation. But where was our promoter?

Eventually he emerged, now looking even paler. For someone who was the 'hardest man in Africa', he was a mumbling mess. He blurted out that it was his entire fault... he had forgotten to book lights! And we had a 20,000 thousand crowd in by now, in complete darkness! "What can we do? What can we do!" We were back on the management team again! "I think what you have to do, Mike, is to tell them that the lights don't work, or there's been a technical problem," I suggested. "Blame the local electricity suppliers, the contractors, the Obong."

"I can't blame the Obong!" he shouted.

"OK! OK! Here's what you do, come clean, and tell them the lights have failed, but give them a pass, and we'll put on the show tomorrow night." I agreed that blaming the Obong was not the best policy. Strange things have happened to white men in jungles.

"Could you make the announcement, Orig?" he asked. He received a swift reply in Welsh and rudimentary Anglo-Saxon English. So off went a nervous Power Mike, thanking me profusely. Jim and I retired to a safe distance expecting trouble. Mike made the announcement and to our sheer astonishment, the entire crowd stood up and politely walked towards the exits to collect their passes for the following night. Not a whimper of protest as they trooped in single file into the night. Astonishing!

Even more bewildering was the audience for the following evening. It seemed to have doubled. Passes had been handed out, but they had run out of them, and so my promoter decided to hand out blank pieces of white paper. You can imagine what happened. Everybody and his uncle in the region seemed to have a pass. A blank piece of paper was the best ticket in town! We'd worked with a gang, in blistering heat all day, to set up adequate temporary lights and generators. Stupid but typical Welshman as I was, by the time I was finished I had a bad case of sunburn, but at least the show was going on. We tested the lights and all was OK. The scene was set. Apart from one item! A warm-up event had been booked – a large female Nigerian dance troupe with band. On came the lights and on came the girls – all of them topless! Amazing! I wish I could have started my shows in Llandudno, Rhyl and everywhere else in this fashion. The dance troupe was rhythmically fantastic in every sense, and had obviously been hand-picked to excite an all-male crowd – they certainly achieved that. But, more importantly, the lights had also alerted all the insects in Nigeria that there was a good night going on in Calabar. The topless girls didn't seem to mind, but these insects were coming in far faster than anything at Heathrow. You couldn't count them – it was a blanket invasion.

My mate, the great wrestler Jim Moser, was from Trinidad. He had impeccable English, which to the Nigerians, who'd been under British rule for years, made him white. But, whatever he was, Jim was a believer in 'evil spirits', and was petrified by insects. In that respect he was certainly in the wrong place at the wrong time. By the time Jim got to the ring, the place had been attacked. The insects were on the mat in their thousands – almost looking like an Axminster carpet covered in crawling things. You didn't know what would bite you, or what wouldn't. In the ring he waved a towel at me, just like a *Titanic* passenger. He could not stand it, and wanted out, and indeed gave way to the local man in the second round. In Blackpool, he would have hammered the man.

It was my turn. These insects were not small – not the sort of gnats that you might see on a warm summer's evening. These were airbus size, all extremely colourful, and probably fascinating on a BBC 2 David Attenborough programme. But, on that night, each time Jim had gone down on the canvas with his opponent, there was blood all over his body – not his, just the corpses of the huge insects. Not only that, there were flying insects buzzing around everywhere. This was a great, big bug carnival. I looked at my opponent, but he was not concerned with the wildlife invasion. He was used to it, and I noticed that the crowd was none too concerned either. Just me – and every time I opened my mouth, it filled with these damned things! What was I to do? I entertained the idea of submitting to my opponent at the first opportunity. That would at least please the locals, and I could escape this insect-infested hell. The bell went. My opponent Hercules was a strong man: this could be a very early submission and, as we crashed around the ring, the mortality rate among the insects was rising at an alarming rate. Round one was over, and I washed myself down and got rid of the corpses with a bucket of water. Suddenly, I was aware that Hercules was coming towards me although the bell hadn't gone for the next round. He was on my back and giving me a good pasting. That annoyed me as much as it delighted the crowd. What else did I expect? He was the local hero – and obviously there were no rules. I decided that he was going to have some jungle medicine of his own returned. I had to wait for an opportunity – but these insects were a flaming nuisance. And that made me even angrier.

Mid-way through the second round he attempted a drop kick on me. It wasn't a good one. He was strong, but technically a novice, and that included being deaf to the bell. He missed completely with the kick, and landed heavily on the canvas. Judging by the crunching noise, a fair number of insects had perished in the process. But he was also dazed and attempted to get up slowly. But, I was on his back in a flash, and I put a fierce 'boston grab' hold on him. I was going to teach him a lesson. He squealed as I put on more and more pressure. Eventually he screamed so loud that Power Mike and one of his mates jumped into the ring and forced me to release. The local man had been defeated.

I was aware of the silence. Not a single voice could be heard, just the constant buzz of the insects. No one moved. The crowd just stared at me. I had heard of what happened to Christian missionaries in the past, and I suddenly forgot about the insects. I still do not know why I did it, or what inspired me. I took hold of the microphone and in English told the crowd that I was the victor – the white man – who had been granted exceptional godly and supernatural powers to overcome all challengers. No black man had ever defeated me, and no black man ever would!

Power Mike translated, and they listened. I got out of the ring, and the crowd quietly parted giving me a path towards the changing rooms. There was not a sound... apart from those bloody insects – and Jim Moser's laughter. That was the problem with taking wrestling shows to foreign places. You simply could not predict what might be on the other side of the curtain.

I was building up a reputation as a travelling showman and, if I accepted every invitation that came my way, I could have been on the road for twelve months a year. It was, or could have been, a decent way of making a living. Fortunately, I became a little more experienced when dealing with some of the foreign operators on the phone. They all wanted big men, some wanted girls, they all promised full houses, great hotels and attractive contracts. I didn't believe a word of it until I had done my research.

My early experiences had taught me a great deal, but I could now narrow it down to one sentence: 'Believe no one, trust no one, and make no promises.' One of my earlier disasters was to accept an invitation to take a show to Sierra Leone. All I knew was that it was in Africa. It just goes to show how innocent and ignorant I was. As soon as we arrived I realised that this was a mistake. This was not an affluent tourist paradise. The little tin sheds on the side of the road were homes to large families and their playground was the street. At our lodgings we were presented with an impeccably wrapped and unopened parcel, which I immediately recognised. It contained the posters I had sent from north Wales to our agent. These, I had been promised, would adorn the entire country by the time we arrived.

There was nothing we could do but postpone, and use the time to drum up publicity. Off we went to do what I seem to have done for most of my life – distribute flyers. At least I wouldn't have north Wales's police on my back. But as soon as we covered one area, we realised that we were being followed and our posters were being torn down. Ironically, it was off to the police station to find out what was going on. And as for our local agent, he hadn't been seen for a long time. It was explained to us that we did not have permission to stage anything unless it had been granted by 'the man'. The man was Mr Justice Donald Macaulay QC. He was Oxford-educated and an English speaker – and in a country with four languages and fifteen other indigenous tribal languages, that news was most welcome. And with a surname like Macaulay, he was bound to be a Scot – a Celt!

But, not quite so. Mr Justice Macaulay was a large man with a very large laugh. He was extremely polite and exuded confidence. Nothing moved in this country without Macaulay's say so. "These people are far too poor to pay for any kind of entertainment," he explained, "no one has work, so they do not have money, and whatever they get, they will spend it on feeding themselves." As a country, Sierra Leone had only been in existence for five years, having been granted independence from Britain. Investment and industry had long disappeared, and for some unknown reason I had accepted an invitation to come here. Where was the damn agent anyway? Mr Justice looked at us, and gently smiled. "I do have a suggestion, but it is entirely up to you. I will arrange for you to have a show here, as long as it is free!" I nearly choked. "But what I will then arrange is for you to put on another show, at the diamond mine, where people do earn money – and good money too! As I said, it is entirely up to you." This man is so kind and generous I thought, until the irony of the situation became clear. A free show in Freetown! And a show at a diamond mine, operated by none other than the smiling QC in front of me. Game, set and match to Macaulay. What an operator! He had become exceptionally wealthy as he was the owner of bars and gaming machines. He also handed out a peculiar form of justice. He was more of an agent than a QC and in one judgment, against diamond thieves, he fined them £3m and then split the court dues between the government and himself – presumably as his legal fees. I did not return to Sierra Leone. There were greener pastures. Not quite an apt phrase perhaps as the desert nations were areas devoid of grass. No matter, because oil revenue can do anything – build skyscrapers, hotels, airports and even purpose-built wrestling arenas.

CHAPTER 10

Fellow Travellers

As a wrestling 'heel' or promoter, I met most of my contemporary British wrestlers – the silent tough ones and the loud-mouth showboats. Most could have kept the country's psychiatric wards busy for decades, but thankfully few were admitted – otherwise they would never have been let out. You would not think that men who could hit, slam, grapple, twist spines and limbs would have to be wet-nursed. But many did.

Some drank, others popped pills or chased women – most just moaned about life in general. Wrestlers are a breed apart and I loved what the wrestling world had to offer, despite the daily hassles: wrestlers are survivors – they have to be since, if truth be told, only a few of them could have made a living anywhere else. So they had to succeed. Many of them were just lazy, demanding slobs – losers – but I do have an overarching admiration for anyone who is prepared to risk life and limb, often without any kind of financial backing to do what they do. They certainly were not insurable. Most were incurable – definitely certifiable.

That was in the days when men needed work. Many a time I would be approached by a collier or steelworker who wanted to wrestle. Sadly their hard, heavy work had already ruptured their limbs and muscles and I had to turn them away. These were undoubtedly hard men, grinning and toothless, who had hewn the rock and been hewn by it. In later years, I wish I could have turned back the clock and hired them all, especially when a young lad boasting 5 GCSEs would turn up wanting to be a wrestler.

The would-be wrestlers had seen the great acrobatic moves on television; they'd seen the adulation and the promotion. They had no idea how much training and preparation was involved before you were allowed into the inner sanctum of wrestling. Jumping from a wardrobe onto a soft bed was no preparation.

And don't tell me that it was all fixed. Just go along to a

wrestlers' reunion, or talk to an old wrestler and see what mental and physical scars he now suffers. The punishment endured secured an early grave for a number of them. Ask Mitzi Mueller, a world-class performer, about what it was like to have three traction operations in hospital and how she had broken nearly every bone in her body over the years.

I'll show you an old wrestler. His face is sculptured, he leans awkwardly. There is a prominent limp and he needs assistance in getting up from his seat to move to a corner where he can hear the conversation. He, or she, will talk of the fights, the characters and of the good old days. But their bent bodies have had to be fixed, sadly.

In wrestling, you give your body to your opponent. It is the first essential lesson that you must learn. You should know your opponents moves inside out, and have trust that he, or she, will never overstep the mark. That is the textbook theory. Unfortunately, a number of the wrestlers I knew and fought didn't seem to be able to read!

Without doubt, the biggest problem I ever had was persuading a wrestler to lose in his home town on the first of a series of wrestling nights. For someone with a championship belt or a title, this was extremely difficult. Try as I would, it was hard to explain that if he lost the first bout, then this would set up a 'revenge' fight at the end of the week and in turn double the gate. Joe Erskine, a former boxer, in front of his home town Cardiff crowd, could not grasp this at all. Some of the wrestlers were so dull that they couldn't remember the instructions. Some would not entertain such a proposal at all – in fact, I don't think Adrian Street ever lost a fight in Wales.

Now the American wrestling stage is a huge production. It is stage-managed, built on storylines and the choreography is immense and completely driven by television angles. The so-called battles, feuds and belt challenges last for months. We now have US centres where wrestlers are trained to speak, challenge, intimidate and pout. It wouldn't surprise me if they were all members of the actors' union, Equity. Can you imagine Haystacks, Klondyke or our lot doing that?

When the fans, or 'punters' as we called them, turned up to shout abuse at the boys, few of them would have realised that these guys and dolls had travelled the length of the country to be there. They'd erected the ring and would probably end up sleeping under it, or in the back of a car or a van after the fight, or driving the nation's motorways to get to the next 'All Star, No Mercy, No Submission, Revenge Wrestling Extravaganza'. I have been banned, stabbed by stiletto heels, hounded by court officials and solicitors, and chased by angry fans, and the pressure of having to be one step ahead – by whatever means – has been constant. But I would not have swapped it for anything else. It is, as my friend Brian Dixon says, 'a poison'.

It was also Brian who kept reminding me that I could not be a wrestler and a promoter at the same time. On reflection and much later in life, I had to accept that this was based on sound judgement, but during those early incredible years of lurching from crisis to success, I was not the most attentive of listeners. And there was nothing like holding court with the boys after a show, to share the tales and lies, with a pint of Guinness or two.

But, wrestlers can be a cantankerous lot. Many didn't like each other for the most trivial of egotistical reasons, although they would spend half their working lives in each other's company. There were real feuds. But I will say this – should they collectively be attacked or threatened by an outsider, then look out! And they did put up with a lot. But that was their job. And it was a living of sorts – £4 a night – in my early days.

Jackie Pallo and Mick McManus were disliked by many, though I suspect that envy caused most of the resentment. They were top stars. And, like it or not, all of us benefited by having them around. Pallo knew everything and had done everything and was a most convincing liar. He even claimed that he'd scaled Everest and had been present at the D-Day landings! He also claimed that the decline of wrestling in this country was entirely due to his retirement.

There were two outstanding 'villains' both in and outside the rings – Bert Assarati and Les Kellet. Assarati had been a formidable wrestler since the 1930s and was still wrestling after the Second World War. He was not a tall man – about five foot six inches – but he weighed sixteen stone and was as strong as an ox, and agile with it. He could carry a piano on his back for a fair distance and he was a fitness fanatic. He wasn't particularly disliked by wrestlers, but he was feared. And the British wrestlers tried to have him banned.

Such was his fame for hurting people that fellow wrestlers avoided him. If they had to fight him, they would demand double the normal fees and, inevitably, eventually, Assarati had to go abroad to find opposition. It is said that he took on ten top martial arts experts in Japan, and beat them all in one day. He also defeated the German 'Giant Gargantuan' – all seven foot two and fifty stones of him. To Assarati, wrestling was a physical science – no fakes, no fixes – all strength and pain. I saw wrestlers turn up to see the posters and when matched against Bert, they would turn around and hoof it back down to the railway station. He was a great technician, but an unforgiving one – especially to those he didn't respect, and there were quite a few of those. He filled his non-wrestling time as a bouncer and doorman. Again, he was fearless, as many a London gangster could testify. In life, and in the ring, he took no prisoners.

Big Daddy, who used to wrestle as Shirley Crabtree – the Blonde Adonis – had just been crowned British champion when Assarati challenged him from the crowd. Asserati wanted the British crown, and no matter how well connected Big Daddy was in Joint Promotions, Bert was desperate for that crown. Big Daddy ran for his life – as would many of us – such was Assarati's reputation. And Big Daddy would had to have run a lot further had he not been the brother of Max Crabtree, the country's biggest promoter at that time.

Towards the end of his career, Assarati was refereed by one Les Kellet. Les was one of nature's total misfits – and a man feared by all. He started wrestling when he was fifty-eight years old. It didn't matter who or what you were, a fellow wrestler or a member of the public, Les was best avoided. He felt no pain and could reduce men to tears. He was, in short, quite detestable, though the public loved him and his antics. He lived with

Margaret, his Irish wife, on a run-down farm on the Yorkshire moors – it was a filthy place with neglected animals. Later be bought a small transport café, frequented by his ducks and geese, but few customers. I picked him up a few times and we travelled hundreds of miles without a word exchanged.

Les had refused to do national service, claiming that he was a conscientious objector and a vegetarian! Thrown into jail, he began a hunger strike, prompting the army to throw uncooked sprouts, turnips and potatoes into his cell! Or so he told me. He then joined the merchant navy. I felt for the man, or men, who had to share quarters with him! I've not met a more stubborn or reclusive individual and, since he was likely to erupt at the slightest provocation, he was given a wide berth. Unfortunately, some members of the public, especially loudmouths in a bar with a woman to impress on their arm, would try and have a go at him. He would bide his time, challenge the loudmouth to some dare of pain endurance, and the end would be an inevitable hospital bed for the challenger.

There was one dare in particular that I remember. Les had the ugliest hands ever: they were always dirty, and more like crab claws than normal hands. He would challenge someone to place their hands in his mouth. It was quite absurd. The offer would be refused, so Les would challenge the man, "If you are a man... " and so on, to put his fingers in the man's mouth. That would be it. Les used his claws and turned them in the stranger's mouth, and then you'd hear the squeals of pain, agony and pleas for mercy. He suffered a serious neck and spine injury once, and after hospital isolation he was advised to take a long holiday in order to recuperate. He spent that time in the gym, analysing how he had been thrown and how he would avoid it happening again.

But he couldn't half wrestle! Unfortunately, he began playing the clown – an act that the ITV commentator Kent Walton thought was funny (Walton knew more about his navel than he did about wrestling). Les was well connected, ironically, to the Grade family, and it was one of them, Michael Grade, who took Saturday afternoon wrestling off the screen, thus decimating the industry. Les was convinced that he should play the clown, and would stroll around the ring as if in a drunken stupor – which sometimes was the case – and then take an opponent apart, literally limb by limb. He would never submit and paid the consequences with broken bones. He'd fall on concrete but would never rub himself down. That would have displayed mental weakness. Whether he took great pleasure in hurting opponents and his fellow professionals, we will never know. I suspect he did, because he really did hurt them with his chops, hits and reels from the ropes, which became trademark winning performances. He also suffered from selective deafness and would never admit to hearing the bell at the end of a round if he had a 'persuasive' submission hold on his opponent. In the ring, he was best avoided.

Outside the ring he was a total pain in the arse. He'd make demands at all hours, and if they were not met he would go absolutely berserk – smashing furniture, shouting obscenities and threatening physical violence. He was disliked by his fellow wrestlers but, if he was on your bill, you invariably had a full house, because the Kellet character and his antics were popular.

If Les Kellet was to be avoided, there were very many you would be glad to see. Quite a few wrestling reunions have been organised in recent years – which is rather strange for a group of men and women who spent years hitting lumps out of each other. Normally, when wrestlers retired or moved away, little was seen or heard of them again, apart from in the local newspaper obituary columns. Grievances were not easily forgotten. But there were exceptions.

I had booked that formidable giant from Texas, Ski Hi Lee for a bout in Bristol and a tour of the West Country. He shouldn't have been in the country at all, but Ski (not one of the world's brighter intellectuals) had arrived from a tour of South Africa where his agent, Bull Heffer was to give him a percentage of the tour's takings in sterling. Ski had flown into London hoping to stay a short while in order to change sterling into dollars, and then fly home to Amarillo in Texas. That was the plan.

Unfortunately, the bag carrying the money was opened at

Heathrow and Ski was asked to explain why he had £16,000 on him in person – which, in the 1970s, was no small change. He tried his best to explain the circumstances, but was detained by Her Majesty's customs for days in a Heathrow cell until his tale was eventually verified by his South African agent. Ski was magic box office and his short stay in the UK was extended to two years. One night, before a show in Bristol, Tony Charles walked in. That was trouble and I knew it.

Tony Charles, a fellow Welshman, was one of the best wrestlers around, having done his apprenticeship fighting in the pubs and dancing halls of the Rhondda. He'd heard that Ski was in town; Ski was a man he much admired and liked, and although he had only just arrived back from Japan himself, he had decided to look up his old mate. They were both world renowned and well-recognised wrestlers. They also had another claim to fame – they were both world-class drinkers as well.

After the show, we went back to the hotel: tales were told and boasts were made. There was a great deal of laughter and numerous bottles containing alcohol were bought. I am not sure when I went to sleep on the floor, but dawn had broken when I awoke and the two of them, clasping a bottle of whisky each, were still going strong. Tony, great man and gifted wrestler, eventually left. Ski and I headed for Penzance and our next show. We had to stop at most pubs en route and when we arrived he walked into a supermarket and emerged with three bottles of whisky – his daily liquid diet!

Not far behind Ski in the wrestling world drinking stakes was my old friend Billy Two Rivers – a real Red Indian chief from the Kahnawake Reservation in Quebec, Canada. Whisky and milk were Billy's weaknesses – morning, noon and night!

Red Indians were banned from entering bars and liquor stores in Canada, unless they carried a licence. When Billy arrived here he was under the impression that he had licence to do what he wanted. A striking figure in the ring, complete with an amazing head-dress, he was a most accomplished wrestler. His main weapon – the tomahawk chop – was best avoided.

Unfortunately, his celebrity status exposed him to taunts

and ridicule. However, he enjoyed the adulation of the women roughing up his feathers and played along, much to the annoyance of their escorts and boyfriends. Inevitably, in response, the accompanying males would get annoyed at all the attention going Billy's way and would begin to argumentatively question his authenticity as a Red Indian. Big mistake!

Billy's father was the tribal chief and Billy would eventually take over the responsibility of representing the reservation and the tribe. He became a respected politician and rights campaigner on behalf of the Canadian Red Indians. Questioning his authenticity was never the brightest of moves. But there are none so brave as those in drink, and having to play second-fiddle to a Red Indian near closing time.

Billy would invite any troublemakers outside to see his war dance. The tomahawk chop would be swiftly and correctly applied, and then the drinking of whisky and milk would resume inside with his chosen company, as if the whole thing had been an advertising interlude. Naturally, his ill-advised challenger would limp into the night with, or without, his female company.

I have little time for nobility or royalty, whose survival depends on succession rather than success. And we have enough noble and royal prats to fill a galaxy. There is, however, one self-proclaimed 'lord' and one 'queen' who deserve my respect, and total admiration. I had no idea that at the time when I was running my annual summer shows in Rhyl, a young wrestling enthusiast was in the audience. Darren Matthews had become obsessed with the sport and would travel from Blackpool to watch and learn. It was in his blood as his grandfather had done a bit of ring time, and young Darren, without any real work prospects, had the drive and determination to make it as a wrestler, and if he trained and put on some weight in the right places, he'd be successful. He watched our shows, which included The Wild Man of Borneo, Crusher Mason and one Adrian Street. We didn't have the services of TV stars in those days, so we had to be inventive – we not only wrestled, we promoted ourselves also. It was a lesson not lost on the young Mr Matthews.

He was to become a superstar as Lord Steven Regal or Lord

William Regal. A bit upmarket from the original Roy Regal name that I gave him as my tag partner! I had a hand in his introduction to the big boys from across the pond – the Extreme Championship Wrestling (ECW), as it was then known. Steven Regal had absorbed the lot in his formative years. He had toured in Europe with Otto Wenz, had worked for myself and Brian Dixon, and had gained respect from all, either as Roy or Steven Regal. He'd worked on his strength, technique and he was a pleasant man to have around.

He even befriended Haystacks, which was no mean feat. He embraced life, and always did what *he* wanted to do. Mind you, there were times when Haystacks could have throttled him outside the ring. Regal was a leg-puller, and Haystacks was often an easy target, especially when Steven was asked to do Haystacks' shopping. The big man hated supermarkets, laundrettes or any place where people would gawk at his six-foot eleven-inch, forty-five-stone frame. Regal would take full advantage of the big man's shyness, and the content of the shopping basket was not always to his liking. It was always "I f****** asked you to buy something, and you bring this f****** garbage." Regal would walk away laughing his head off, while the big man drowned in his own expletives.

But the call for Regal came. The ECW was coming to the UK for a tour, and were recruiting British wrestlers. They wanted Steven who was by now established and had a credible reputation. It was his making – but, subsequently, the move to the United States after becoming a WWE superstar much later was also his downfall.

He fought for me a few times on the road in Ireland and Scotland. He was always willing to do anything: erect the rings and take tickets at the door. There was nothing he liked more than touring our Celtic countries and enjoying the beautiful countryside. But, suddenly, he was catapulted into the US big time – the glitz, the television, the storylines and, above all else, the promotion of it. The Americans are talkers. They thrive on claims, threats and basic bull. The wrestling itself is secondary to the 'big talk'. Can you imagine the likes of Les Kellet, Haystacks or Klondykes with microphone in hand, holding an audience? They'd have cleared the halls.

Regal could talk the talk, and I knew he would make it. I also knew that he was on the small side for the American ring, although he was six foot four inches. That would inevitably require short-cut methods to build up bulk – and that would mean steroids and whatever else was available in the 'sweetshop'. I thought he might be intelligent enough not to follow the familiar paths known to us all.

There was no doubt that Regal was one of our most successful exports and, along with Dave 'Fit' Finlay, the British Bulldogs and Adrian Street, the reputation of British wrestlers abroad was fantastic during this period. But, for Regal, there was a price to pay. Here he was, up there with the best, a great guy, good company and a worthy 'lord', but he was the architect of his own downfall. Following an amazing start, his later tales of alcohol and drugs make sorry reading. Regal could wind-up any audience and orchestrate them by acting as an English 'toff'. In time, he did eventually see off his weaknesses. He was a great ambassador for British wrestlers, for all of us. Not only that, he became a highly respected wrestling administrator, though his fondness for keeping reptiles left me totally cold.

But, in terms of being a showman, he was upstaged by one exceptional Welshman. I would say that though, wouldn't I? The Beynon colliery boy from Brynmawr, near Ebbw Vale, was something else. The nicest thing he ever called me was the 'ogre of north Wales'. I must assume he meant it as a compliment, since I helped train his partner – the lovely Linda – his one-time valet who was to become his wrestling business associate and wife. Adrian Street added a new dimension to wrestling. Let me get one thing straight, which is not easy when talking about him, because he intentionally became *the* 'queen bitch' of the ring. He was a fierce and the most inventively talented performer – one of the best, and as many an opponent found out, he could be ruthless!

From childhood he had been fascinated with dressing up: as a Red Indian, a pirate – anything that would attract attention.

It was probably escapism, since life in Brynmawr after leaving secondary school and then spending two years underground was not that interesting. Picture him, then, in these outrageously flamboyant costumes, with full make up, blowing kisses towards his opponents and dancing provocatively to his chosen tracks. You can imagine how this would go down in the redneck communities of America. He worked on being outrageous – a one man, or should I say, a one man and his wife marketing team. It was outstanding! All the more astonishing then, that he was forty-one years old before going to America after achieving a high-profile career in Europe and elsewhere, beginning as 'Tarzan Boy Jonathan', 'Nature Boy' and the 'World's Youngest Professional Wrestler', and facing the likes of Jackie Pallo and Mick McManus when still in his teens!

He was big time in Europe, but was made for America – the perfect target 'heel' for its audiences. The more they hated him and his sequins, the more he worked at it, and when I saw him on the large-scale promotions, I doffed my cap to him and Linda: they'd conquered the American marketing gurus in their own backyard. A far cry from the Rhyl summer shows! But I remember him saying that, for all the razzmatazz of the American circuit, the posing of grudge matches, the endless variety of belts, British wrestling at that time had the best technicians in the world.

One of those technicians was Johnny Kincaid, who inherited two of Adrian's children when he married Adrian's first wife. Johnny was a black wrestler who dyed his hair a marketable blond. He deserved his success, as his early life being one of seven children, consisted of shuttling between various families, courts and detention centres. In his early days he was a boxer, and he had followed my trail, beginning in the West Country travelling boxing booths operated by Mickey Kiely.

I remember the time when he caught the wrestling bug. I had booked him as a novice for a show in Pembrokeshire. He was to be the proverbial lamb to the slaughter. But the Welsh audiences warmed to him, not only in Pembroke, but Carmarthen, Caerphilly, Llanelli and Swansea. They applauded the loser, and Johnny never got over that. He embraced the adulation, especially when I told him he had a 'baby face'! He went on to be a great 'heel'. Unfortunately, for those in the audience who wanted to have a go at him, Johnny did sometimes have a short fuse.

My daughter, Tara Bethan, owes her life to Dave 'Fit' Finlay, one of the best we have produced on this side of the Atlantic, and who now trains America's top wrestlers. Dave was on one of our Irish tours, and inevitably there had been one of those last-minute changes of venues. It was a common challenge. A change of location always meant a dash to another village or venue, not only for us, but usually also the punters – there would always be an almighty rush to get into the hall. It happened too frequently, and in fairness the wrestlers took their bodyguard responsibilities quite seriously. I remember Dave 'Fit' Finlay, a great wrestler, picking Tara, my baby daughter up from the ground and holding her above an excited and menacing Irish throng. Otherwise, a serious accident could have occurred. Thank you, Dave!

Haystacks, too, was not shy in coming forward to do a bit of babysitting. Thank goodness Tara was too young to understand what he might have been telling her. Probably something to do with him being a friend of Paul McCartney and Frank Sinatra. He could talk to trees, that great man! And he could sleep. Anywhere! I remember a booking arranged by an agent in Oman called Vergese. Naturally, this involved a flight to Oman, and it always took time to convince Haystacks to fly. On this particular Gulf Air flight, the plane was very full and I had to negotiate a place for Haystacks where the cabin crew would usually sit. He called me every expletive under the sun for taking him on that plane, to a place where he didn't want to go – and why were we going there anyway? He called me a Welsh bastard about twenty times before the plane had taken off. It got worse during the flight because he couldn't sleep.

"Turn this f****** plane around, I don't want to go. You are just a Welsh bastard. Give me some tablets." I happened to have some very strong tablets for a health condition, and I offered him two. "I want four of them, otherwise I am not coming with you," said Haystacks, ignoring the fact that we were already 30,000 feet above France at the time.

He accepted the two tablets complaining that two Smarties would have been more effective.

We arrived in Oman. It was early in the morning and Haystacks was moaning like a cow about to deliver a calf. All he wanted to do was to get to a bed. Off he went, whereas Vergese, the agent, and I headed out to the football stadium where the show was due to be staged that night. It was about 6 a.m. What is it about agents? As soon as we arrived at the stadium I could see that there were no lights and no PA system. Vergese looked at me in horror and I looked back at him, in disbelief. We spent the next four hours phoning all the electrical and sound companies around in an effort to solve the problem.

Hours later I returned to the hotel to get some sleep. As we approached the hotel, there were hundreds of kids milling around, and they were all very excited. Inside the hotel foyer there were even more kids, and obviously there was something going on. I heard it first – then I saw it. Sprawled on a sofa in the middle of the hotel foyer was Haystacks, fast asleep, and drowning the place with the fiercest, loudest snores and snorts known to mankind. The kids had never seen or heard anything like it. From somewhere, a reporter and press photographer arrived. I tried my best to wake him up. I shook him, shouted at him and somehow got him to stir. Then he awoke and, with a mighty lunge and huge roar, went for the reporter, picking him up with one hand. The poor fellow must have been three feet off the ground and was being barked at by Haystacks in very colourful language. The kids fled in fright whilst the snapper took a picture of his airborne colleague. Haystacks was awake, and in Oman.

Good 'heels' and the 'hated' wrestlers had to work hard at their trade. For most it didn't come naturally and it would take years to develop into a great heel. The crowd hated Haystacks as soon as they looked at him. But one man, a heel, stood above the rest. He was a Canadian by the name of Mighty John Quinn. By the time he had reached our shores, he'd won titles and belts by the dozen in the World Wrestling Federation events and had fought the best. His world title fight with Bruno Sammartino had packed out Madison Square Gardens. Quinn was an Ontario monster – six foot six inches and twenty stone with attitude. But he was something of an independent eccentric. After working for Otto Wenz in Germany at one of the big festivals, he'd arrived in Britain. Such was his reputation that he was able to walk into Joint Promotions and state his fee. They took him on and immediately put him on our television screens.

He wanted to be regarded as a heel in this country, and immediately placed his marker. I remember watching him on television, and I nearly fell out of my chair. It was in Hemel Hempstead I think, at a pre-Cup Final transmission. As soon as he got into the ring, he took hold of the mike and told the packed audience what a bunch of cowards the British had been, especially during the Second World War. His father, a Canadian war pilot, had told him that if he ever wanted to see a nation of yellow belly bastards, England was the place to go. He went on and on, and there was uproar, and the Mighty John Quinn was, from that moment on, more despised than any wrestler I have ever come across. Job done! He put the 'H' in Heel.

John Quinn, with Tony St Clair, Haystacks, Dave 'Fit' Finlay, Mike 'Rollerball' Rocco and Adrian Street were all big business. And they all came over to the independent promoters and were immediately welcomed and embraced. What a cocktail they were. Each had their idiosyncrasies. They were individuals – in the extreme.

But how do you explain to a man who had fought the best wrestlers around in the world's largest halls and stadiums, and who was more than happy to bring himself and his family to north Wales that they'd be staying in a converted bread van parked on Rhyl promenade? This was a man who wanted space, and liked nothing better than to roam around the Denbighshire moors and the Snowdonia mountain ranges. He thrived on scenery, space and peace. Thankfully, we had a lot of it in Wales. And, thankfully, we eventually found him a holiday cottage, because life in the bread van was rather basic.

Yes, this was the Mighty John Quinn. He knew that I was also looking for a new house and location too. I wanted a remote Welsh-speaking area, not far from my business base in Rhyl, and strangely enough he was the one who found it. It was a somewhat run-down old farmhouse in a village called Llansannan. We have lived there ever since. Quinn had read my mind – he understood what I required, and we became great friends.

When he finally decided it was time to take his family home to Canada, I lost the company of a genuine friend, and the friendship of Linda, his wife. In our business, such relationships were rare. I had even bailed him out from a Sheffield police station because some idiotic Cardiff policemen thought he looked like the Yorkshire Ripper.

The road shows were planned as well as they could be. The wrestlers would spend weeks or months in each other's company – fight each other every night, and drink together during the day. You had to carefully choose your wrestlers. Some of those road shows, especially in Ireland and Scotland, were long and challenging. At the beginning, we would all sleep in the ring van, and if that didn't bond people nothing would. A little later, we could afford the local B&Bs or guest houses, but these struggled to accommodate the likes of Haystacks, Klondyke Bill and anyone else over six foot. The size of the rooms were not the only problem, you also had to contend with a few over-sized egos as well. I think what I did on those road shows, rightly or wrongly is now history.

CHAPTER 11

My Personal Column

I HAVE NEVER BEEN afraid to voice an opinion or two. Wendy and Tara would claim that I have an opinion on everything. I could well be described as a proud nationalist, but my political leanings towards either the left or the right have mainly been determined by the weather and how I felt when I got up that morning. I wouldn't call myself a political activist – there are too many people far cleverer than me to fill such positions, but I am incensed by injustices and things that should be put right.

So, when an invitation came to write a weekly Welsh-language personal column for the *Daily Post*, I thought it quite right that I should accept. It was called 'Siarad Plaen', the English translation being 'plain talking'. After all, it was only an extension of my constituency surgery sermons in various pubs throughout the country! And those on the wrestling circuit would have spent many an hour listening to my opinions on life.

The logistics of writing a column and then sending it via the Internet to the paper were quite beyond me. I would spend a few days thinking of a theme or subject; surprisingly, they didn't come that easily at the beginning and my telephone directory of friends was well thumbed when I was stuck! But, gradually, not a news bulletin would pass without something getting under my skin.

It was arduous work writing it and then handling it over to Wendy or Tara to complete it with amendments, lines crossed out, terrible punctuation and don't mention the grammar! They would put it into some sort of shape and send it by computer. As ever, I could not have done without them. You will have gathered by now that organisation was not my forte, and my life has been guided by two defining principals – Wendy and Tara!

In recent years, I have been surrounded by television and media people. You know the types – university-educated, opinionated, highly thought of (by themselves, naturally) and largely without common-down-to-earth-sense. Not a hardened hand amongst them. Not all of them would fit into that category – a few became genuine friends, but I would like nothing better than to take opposite viewpoints, just to make the conversation a little livelier. And if they'd argue a point, I would become even more outraged. It was my good fortune to come across people from a wide spectrum of backgrounds and interests. Even the odd politician could be considered an ally, but they, like me, had a primary ability to talk, not to listen!

Here was an opportunity of filling a weekly pulpit, with the world and its problems as my brief. Not bad for a boy who had no scholastic future at Llanrwst Grammar! Fortunately, my world was confined to Wales. Had I ventured beyond, and in English, I am sure, courtesy of the libel laws of the country, my column would have been withdrawn. In the Welsh language, I knew I could get away with murder – or launch a literary submission hold on the unsuspecting public.

One of my priorities was to get at those south-Walian Cardiff Bay satisfied egos who, after devolution, thought they ran my country. Those in charge of protecting the Welsh language came in for stick as well. The policy of making my backyard a bilingual one was to be applauded, but in one column I had a good old rant against someone in a Mold shop who had translated 'deodorants' into *diaroglyddion*. I am sure that no one in Ysbyty Ifan had a clue what it meant – I certainly didn't. Some of the roads signs are laughable and confusing and it underlines that the language, which has been here for centuries, does not lend itself to trendy translations thought up by someone with a Welsh degree. The *Western Mail* and *Daily Post* carry acres of governmental and local authority notices, all of them academically translated – but they are written in a language that is alien to most of us. A complete waste of space and time! Far better to spend the money on keeping village schools open in Wales.

If I ever had the opportunity of highlighting hard men, then I would. Lauding people like the south Wales valleys boxers – Tommy Farr, Jim Driscoll, Freddy Welsh and Jimmy Wilde – was always productive territory. Can you imagine 100,000 people turning up in Cardiff for the funeral of Jim Driscoll? It happened, because these men were gods! And who could ever forget Tommy Farr's immortal phrase when referring to his birth place, 'There are no angels in Tonypandy!' I admired and wrote about another Rhondda product, Roy Paul, the ex-captain of Wales and Manchester City, who enjoyed a couple of pints with his mates before playing and went home after a distinguished career to work as a lorry driver in the valleys. Roy Paul was a cruncher of a tackler and a hard leader of men. Not for him the distraction of WAGs, fast cars and Lego mansions. I admired people who grafted for their living.

But not the Irish tinkers. Oh no! I read that the Limerick Council, with the blessing of the Irish government, was about to launch some do-good initiative of building new houses for the travelling tinkers. No doubt a strategy promoted by that other waste of a fortune, the European Union, to support the tinkers. They were the very people who had attacked one of our shows at the Rose of Tralee Festival, which featured the Mighty Chang. That developed into a mass brawl between our wrestlers and the mob. The incident prompted a furious article on my part, about those who think that life owes them a living. The Irish are my favourite people (second to the Welsh) – but not their tinkers!

And it wasn't just the politicians who came under scrutiny, but also the Welsh sporting authorities, including soccer and rugby. The problem had always been geography. Caernarfon and Chester are far more relevant to north Wales than Cardiff will ever be. That road between north and south – the A470 – is largely routed on the old cattle drovers' routes, and should have stayed as such. You can just about complete a return journey from Caernarfon to Cardiff in a day, but it is not recommended. Even the politicians agree, and that is why they established their own personal airline from Cardiff to Anglesey, a service that attracted substantial public funding. But, it is predominantly used by the politicians and their officials as a 'private' jet. Little wonder that it was comically quoted as being 'Ieuan's Air', after Ieuan Wyn Jones, the Anglesey AM and deputy minister of the Welsh Assembly.

It was regularly claimed in the Cardiff-published *Western Mail* that rugby was our national sport. Now that would really get me going. Utter bloody nonsense, though I had little time for the players who wore the Welsh soccer shirt either, who tended to withdraw their services at the slightest excuse, having tripped over their weekly pay packets when going for goal. But I was envious of rugby's social life, where the village club was the focus of the community, especially in south and west Wales. The club in those villages meant only one club – and that inevitably belonged to rugby.

The *Western Mail* paper is proclaimed as the 'national newspaper of Wales'. Again, complete nonsense! It does not sell in north Wales, hardly mentions anything of note in north Wales and few of the Thomson Foundation or Cardiff school of journalists have ever ventured beyond Pontypridd. If there is mention of north Wales people in it, invariably it is found in the obituary columns. That is my opinion.

The paper did, however, give prominence to the dealings of the Football Association of Wales – a body that has aggravated me over the years. For several years I was convinced that you had to be over seventy years old to join and had to have the added qualification of having NOT played the game at any respectable level. Naturally, with a weekly column, the FAW was a productive field for my 'constructive criticism'. Not that any of my comments would have influenced anything. In fact, I can solemnly declare that not one of my columns changed public opinion towards the FAW, since most agreed with me in the first place!

As for the England players, I devoted several column inches to the subject of David Beckham, a lion in sheep's clothing, if I ever saw one. And as for those who earn obscene weekly wages for kicking a ball, I would have liked to see them tackle Nantlle Vale's 'Tarw' or 'Commando', who would have had them for breakfast, lunch and tea!

I had to be careful about criticising Welsh television, as the S4C channel had been very supportive of wrestling. But there were times when making jam tarts in Welsh, and watching endless unfunny and uninteresting programmes would send me spare, and the writing hand started twitching. I'm afraid that even this channel, in its attempt to please everyone, has failed to embrace its true audience and does not have an identity other than being transmitted in Welsh. You'd be forgiven, when watching S4C, to think that Wales was totally populated by well-intentioned academics, politicians and opinionated spokespeople sitting on comfy sofas, interviewed by sons of the manse! Good comedy has been rare, and understanding sports commentaries requires a degree in inventive Welsh.

I am told that reality television is the thing these days. Really! It obviously is cheap to produce, by producers and presenters who have not tasted real life, and is an expensive waste of time to watch. Wrestlers know a lot about reality television. There's nothing much else to do if you have a broken ankle or leg! So the *Daily Post* was my personal pressure cooker, with the valve opened once a week. I did not seek to offend, but there were times I felt a need to provoke. I did campaign for the re-introduction of the birch. Oh so non-politically correct.

Everyone, including me, talks about a lack of respect amongst our youngsters and there is nothing like a little bit of discipline to correct matters. When young wrestlers came to me, they were told in no uncertain manner what I expected from them in training. This wasn't always accepted, and if not, they did not last long. A vast number of the younger generation are raised to think that life or the state owes them a living. All of these views found a place in the weekly column.

I objected strongly to the removal of the Gideon's Bible from our hotels and guest-houses, and the removal of the Christian Cross from the country's crematoriums. People do have their own creeds and faith, so I expect them to respect mine.

Along came Mr Tony Blair and his side-kick Alistair Campbell. We were told, beyond doubt, that Saddam Hussein had those weapons of mass destruction – but eventually none could be found. We went to war on that basis, and on that basis I went to print to say that Mr Blair was not convincing – he would never have made a wrestling promoter.

CHAPTER 12

Wales

FORGIVE ME, BUT TO me, Wales is essentially the land of Wendy my wife and daughter Tara Bethan, who was born on the 8th of December 1983. Wendy has been friend, advisor and counsellor. She has travelled the length and breadth of the country, organising our lives and keeping me sane. She has been witness to my misdemeanours and dealings. She keeps her own counsel, whereas I have fought councils!

Tara became a wrestling groupie in her nappies and I have fond memories of the wrestlers being her chaperone at the Irish wrestling shows, and I have already chronicled the debt I owe to 'Fit' Finlay. Tara has followed a career as a successful singer and actress, having been groomed in local and national Eisteddfod competitions. Whereas she is culturally talented, I suspect we share the same temperament, which I am not altogether convinced is a desirable inheritance.

But to see her perform on the sort of stages that I could never grace, gives me astonishing pleasure and pride. I look at her sing in leading roles, and wonder was *this* the baby that was held in the arms of Giant Haystacks and Dave 'Fit' Finlay while I was dong my thing in controlling the mad herds of good Irish people who wanted to get into a wrestling hall?

Without these two women I do not know what I would have done. They have been my rock. I don't think that Wendy had a degree in psychiatry, counselling or avoidance of insolvency. But with her common sense, and despite the dinner plates that sometimes became airborne, we were an incredible tag team. In wrestling terms 'we survived' the lot, together.

There is no better sight than travelling home on the A5 and seeing the mountains of Snowdonia on the horizon. They stand defiant, and have nurtured defiant people. I have heard the Scots talk about this, the Irish too, but whenever I returned to Wales and saw those mountains, nothing else mattered. The peaks and contours have defined and shaped our history, and therefore mine. It was always a comfortable magical feeling and a lot of weight would be taken off my shoulders.

Wales is a diverse mixture of rural and urban people. It has changed immensely during my time. But, not all of it for the good. There was innocence in our communities when I was young. I was surrounded by farmers and labourers, quarrymen and miners, institutions such as chapels, social clubs and community events and it all cemented a bond between locals. Everyone knew each other, and the offer of help was never far away. We shared our joy, celebrations and disasters. We played and ran in streets, and in those days obesity was unheard of. We were allowed to explore, talk to strangers, swim in rivers, and if you were lucky enough to have one, we could listen to the wireless and to people with distant accents.

Now we live in a multi TV channel culture, indoctrinated by America. We sit for hours in front of computers, and you can order anything from your armchair. We are becoming the 'same'. The only division between us is how much you earn and the comforts around you, whether or not you play golf, and where you have booked to go on holiday. Even our pubs, once the social centres, are shutting down. We now have community organisations, and a Communities First funding scheme. I was not aware in Ysbyty Ifan that I belonged to a 'community'. Our community was made up of the first names of peoples who lived in Number 7, 4, 11, and so on, or the occupation of whoever lived there.

We have sportsmen as idols, many of them highly skilled, but who would not survive in the robust and uncompromising battles of old. I am absolutely sure they would not have coped with a soggy leather ball! Sometimes I think ordinary players have been catapulted into superstardom before they have grasped the GCSEs of the game. Television and tabloids, and the sensationalist reporting have much to blame. A WAG in our league was someone who washed your kit!

We've become soft, and have passed too many laws to protect

those who, in some cases, will not protect or have earned the right to protect themselves. Prevention rather than 'creation' is the modern creed. I despair at what has happened to my Wales. Call me a misguided idealist, but I have always been drawn to those who can fend for themselves and have not been reliant on the state. The mines have closed and have been replaced by welfare benefit offices. The steel industry has been decimated, to be replaced by call centres offering life insurances in dead-end areas. Screens have replaced books. Kids 'cut and paste' essays, can't manage a shop till or pocket money without a calculator. We pay restaurant bills by a machine being brought to your table by a waitress. There's no chat, except, "it's slow tonight, sorry about this".

The centres of villages and towns are now boarded up. Tesco, Asda and Morrison's have given birth to scores of charity shops, and our ministers and vicars are in sole charge of parishes, rather than chapels and churches. I fear for the language of Wales. We have coped so far with the challenge of people moving to Wales for the quiet life. To be honest some of our communities have been energised by their arrival. The newcomers have confidence and presence, whereas the Welsh have become accustomed to servility. I was inspired by a speech made by Gwynfor Evans, the then president of Plaid Cymru, at a meeting I attended many years ago with my great friend Huw Sel in Beddgelert. He gave me his vision of Wales as a nation, and from that night on I have carried that independent defiance. He was the man who threatened to fast to death unless Wales was given its own Welsh-language television channel. Even Maggie Thatcher had to bow to him. Great man! If only my fellow countrymen had an ounce of his confidence, we would now be living in a better place.

But the Welsh language now faces a far more sinister challenge, and I suspect that this is true of indigenous culture in other parts of the world. The language of the computer age is predominantly English, or American. It is taking over and our kids are able to manipulate electronic gadgets before they can speak. Computers do not have accents, dialects or local sayings – they have created a technical language that five-year-olds understand, but fifty-year-olds don't.

No matter the strength of political opposition, no matter how many cultural initiatives there are, our language in Wales, my language, will cease to exist, because how on earth can we compete with something I do not understand – cyberspace. I have admired those who have fought for the language, and have supported their actions, but the new-age enemy is, I fear, beyond them. I wish it wasn't. And my English friends had better pull their socks up too – the language of kings is being Americanised.

And whereas I am immensely proud of our heritage, I also have a fear that we are turning our country into a national museum. Communities that are lumbered with derelict buildings are too ready to turn them into publicly grant-funded unsustainable heritage centres and museums. We need a vibrant Wales, a living one. We now have heritage trails, which were once the economic thoroughfares of our communities. The entire bloody country is being turned into a World Heritage site by those who can't think of anything else to do with it. I hate it all!

We need the Wales I enjoyed as a child, as did my heroes, the princes and the poets. I never tired of reading and learning the works of Cynan, T H Parry-Williams, Gwenallt and many more. They were inspired by the raw beauty of the country and its people and, in turn, they inspired me. The only way I could shut up Haystacks going on about his beloved Ireland was to recite some poetry from the land of Cynan!

I became involved in a number of television programmes, and was thrust into an industry that was alien to me as a wrestling promoter. It was far too disciplined for me, far too technical, but it did give me the opportunity, at one stage, of being the only UK promoter to have wrestling on TV. Can you imagine the complications of trying to explain to Big Daddy or Adrian Street what a count was in Welsh!

I enjoyed the company of young and talented people, especially when I could work through the medium of Welsh. Most were welcoming, enthusiastic and talented. Some were annoyingly snobbish, elitist and worthy of a good kick up the backside. What did I know about television production when things went wrong? I would suggest bending the rules, if they could produce a result! Some of the executives would remind me at times of American wrestlers – bullocks looking in the mirrors and seeing bulls!

I enjoyed immensely being fellow compère of a programme called *Y Cymro Cryfa* (The Strongest Welshman). It was transmitted for three years, presented by the excellent and talented Emyr brothers, Arthur and Dafydd. Here was a collection of really strong men from farm-labouring stock, quite a few Welsh rugby internationals, and the odd weightlifter. I added a few of my wrestlers as well! Generally, the wrestlers did not fare very well. The obstacles and weights to be lifted were not to their liking. Strangely, apart from one, they were no competition for the naturally strong competitors. But, at least it was a trial of strength, and that, since the Ysbyty Ifan days, has always fascinated me.

Again, I tried to convince the producer of the programme to bend the rules a little, so as to favour some of my boys. Some of them were huffing and puffing after the first challenge. Admittedly, they were puffed up to the eyeballs, if you know what I mean – after all, this was filmed during the day at agricultural shows, before an audience and in natural light! It did nothing to my credibility as a promoter to see them fail. But, alas, there was no changing the producer's mind, and I held it against him, though with some heavily disguised respect. I don't like being beaten!

I did find other producers, who spoke with forked tongues – in Welsh and English! These generally tended to be BAs. In other words 'Bugger All' from the grand educational universities of Bangor and Aberystwyth. Conveyor-belt graduates. Some had been promoted or appointed either through who they knew, or who they were related to, and who they had sucked up to.

Unfortunately, in an emerging industry, there were far too many of them and gradually, after so much promise, the S4C channel has delivered the kind of programmes they want to see, and not the programmes people want to watch! It is worrying, since S4C is a hugely viable tool in promoting Wales, the language and its culture, but seems to be adrift in mediocrity. It began with so much vitality but, by trying to please all interests in an ever competitive world, it has suffered and fallen short of its goals. It is not the Wales I wanted.

Nor did I envisage what devolution would bring. I campaigned for it and spoke for it, and thanked the good people of Carmarthenshire for their crucial votes in giving us a Welsh Assembly. It was a new dawn, but in reality what we have created are layers upon layers of bureaucrats, committees and officialdom. We read more legislation documents than literature.

We wanted work and factories, but have ended up with waste and public funding. Political correctness – now there's a contradiction – has changed our language. What we sometimes think, we dare not utter. And it is our fault. We lack the confidence of a nation. Ireland has it, primarily because of the sea providing defence and controllable isolation. What if Wales had been an island? Unfortunately, the reality is that Westminster houses the ruling bull mastiffs, and Cardiff Bay is a kennel for yapping Welsh corgis!

I was proud to be installed as a member of the Eisteddfod Gorsedd. It is an honour for any Welshman to wear the robes of the bardic circle. So I joined what some would call the elite of Welsh society, poets, writers, musicians, academics, media and sporting personalities – me, the boy who had no future in Ysbyty Ifan! I wasn't quite sure why I was invited. Maybe they had misspelt someone else's name. It wouldn't have been because of wrestling, or my contribution to Welsh business ethics, or fair play on the football fields of Wales. When you join you are expected to show respect and dignity during the ceremonies. So I apologise now for wearing flip-flops under the robes, but my feet were killing me. I took as my bardic name, which is part of the Gorsedd tradition, the title of Orig Pehalwan (fighter) – the name given to me in Pakistan.

I don't know how many times I have been on television, imploring the big youngsters of Wales to take up wrestling. I must confess that I have tried to persuade rugby players, labourers and weightlifters in various parts of Wales to take up the profession.

A few had a go at it in my Rhyl garage. And then came along a young man from Tremadoc. Not only was he six foot six inches tall and weighing twenty stone, but he was Welsh speaking as well!

I took him under my wing, and I think he will surpass anything that I have ever achieved in the sport. His career might not be so interesting or challenging, but I think and hope that Barri Griffiths will raise the Welsh wrestling flag to greater heights. He's already heading for the USA and the WWE. I also harboured a huge ambition of making it in the USA, but it wasn't to be, so instead I made it up.

I told people that I had auditioned for the WWE in Madison Square Gardens, and it was the big chief himself, Vince McMahon, who had given me the title of 'El Bandito'. With long sideboards and a healthy black moustache, I looked the part of a Mexican. I said the story so often that I think I believed it in the end. But, sadly, like the Irish birthplace of Haystacks, it was pure fiction, befitting a profession totally dependent on image, heels and merchants of violence. No doubt that my prodigy Barri, now Mason Ryan, will be given some other brand name as well.

Barri was called Goliath on the *Gladiators*, the ten-foot Celtic warrior on our shows, but in the United States I wish it could be Llywelyn ein Llyw Olaf, or Owain Glyndŵr. I would love to see big-mouth Mac Mahon get his tongue around that! What Ryan Giggs did for Welsh soccer and Gareth Edwards did for Welsh rugby, Barri could do for wrestling. If he doesn't, he will have to answer to me! El Bandito.

Tributes

MARK 'ROLLERBALL' ROCCO

My dear friend Orig was ahead of his time. I'd known him since I was a teenager, since my father, Jim Hussey, had also worked with him. My kids also loved having Orig and Wendy around, as Orig could and would recite poetry and quote great sayings at the drop of a hat. He was a literate wrestler, an entertainer, a rare specimen whose grunts and moans were the order of the day. He would also take great interest in our children's progress and interests. And that interest wasn't just confined to us. He was interested in people. On the road he could shout and berate, in colourful language, with the best of them – but in friendly or domestic company, he was attentive and generous. He'd been 'groomed' in life's challenges for a long time before he took to wrestling.

I knew he was a tough and robust man, and I heard many times of his battles on the football fields of Wales, with referees in particular. Then there was his baptism of fire in the fairground boxing booths. But to prove a point or to bring a conversation to an end, he would aptly quote Yeats, Shakespeare, Chaucer, Oscar Wilde or Dylan Thomas. Extraordinary!

Orig had a long-term burning ambition to produce a 'dream team' of wrestlers; he handled and promoted some of the best but, unfortunately, not all at the same time. Haystacks, Klondyke Bill, Adrian Street, Dave 'Fit' Finlay, Tony St Clair, Mighty John Quinn and many, many more have been part of the Orig tours and road shows. To realise his ambition of having that team, he would have had to be a negotiating diplomat. He certainly wasn't that, not by a million miles. But what Orig was, was a born grafter and fighter and sometimes, I suspect, he enjoyed being in adversity.

I left Joint Promotions to join Orig – I had that much respect for him. One of the primary reasons for this was that he was a man who was putting something back into the business, and not milking it. Brian Dixon shared that same vision, although they differed as to how to achieve it. Orig would encourage the local Rhyl or north Wales lads to have a go, because nothing would have pleased him more than to have a local Welsh wrestler in the stable. It was his dream. And in his final days he may have found one in Barri Griffiths. I do hope so, but it is a heavy load on Barri, because Orig will watch every step.

I would leave the 'big time' – an 80,000-capacity filled stadium in Japan at the weekend – only to travel with Orig to village halls in Ireland during the week, and then return to the USA or Japan. That was the deal, I could do Japan and the United States, as long as he could have me for the Irish trips, Wales, Scotland and the West Country on the Monday! And life was never dull! He did things that no other promoter would dream of doing. Whether it was a big show or a village hall stint, his attitude was always the same. It mattered little to him whether I had been at Madison Square Gardens the week before, as long as I was in Donegal for his show on Monday! And dare you be late!

But wherever we went, he always seemed to sack me! "You are f****** fired," and then you waited for the call to confirm the next show. "But I am fired, Orig," I would protest. "Listen here; I will decide when you are fired." All this, at a time when I was top of the bill and in demand with other promoters and TV companies in the United States and worldwide. Life with Orig was one roller-coaster, a life-enhancing experience.

One Orig sacking experience in particular deserves a mention. It was in Ireland. I had wrestled in a huge Japanese event; it could have been a world title, the night before (given time zones). We were quite accustomed to changing in the Irish toilets on Orig's tours, but at this venue, there was a hall with 'artist' changing rooms. One room had a big 'star' sign on it, but the Irish caretaker told me, in no uncertain manner, that the star room was for the local school dancers who were performing during the wrestling. I did make a stink, and protested that I was the star and that was why the tickets had been sold, so I should be allowed the use of the facility.

Then, the inevitable Orig call. "You are fired, there are no f****** superstars in this company!" Do not tell me that he was not a man of the people. I know, and I respected and loved him, and will always love him for that. When I did my wrestling apprenticeship in Germany, France, Holland and Pakistan, I didn't realise I was following Orig's footsteps. He was a student of wrestling and its experiences. Unlike the money grabbers, he wanted the business to survive, and he was one of its survivors. I wish he could call me now and sack me again.

ADRIAN STREET – THE EXOTIC ONE
When I look back at the scrapes he got into and the things he did to get out of them, I've just got to laugh. He was an outstandingly inventive rogue, top drawer – there is no doubt about that. He would do anything to survive. The only rules that he would recognise were the ones that could be broken! I am not sure how many times he was taken to court by Joint Promotions for copyright infringements, and as for his successful WWF and WWE lookalike and tribute shows – I don't think he opened the post in the morning. Inventive? Yes! Outrageous? Yes! A character? Most certainly! And did we enjoy working for him and Wendy? Yes, indeed!

He would put up posters in various towns with the names of the top wrestlers of the time in huge letters – McManus, Pallo, Street, Haystacks – all of them, but none of them his. If you looked carefully at the small print, it would say something like, "The above have been invited!" Then, at the start of the show, he would address the audience and berate the named stars for being unprofessional and cowardly for not turning up. "Who do these TV stars think they are," he'd shout, and then introduce his wrestlers who were a few planets away from being household TV names.

But if there was a buck to be made Orig was around. He'd put on anything if he thought it might pull in a crowd – even belly dancers! I remember having to do two shows in Cardigan in a day, one early evening, another late at night. I made more money that day than in a month with Joint Promotions.

He was my saviour. I was with Joint Promotions, but the Crabtrees were treating us like financial idiots: they paid us little, but made a fortune for themselves. When El Bandito, with his so-called north Wales Mexican moustache and a wily Welsh smile, came along offering me half the gate to join him, I was there. And off we went – everywhere – and others followed too. But the trips to Ireland were legendary.

I had started to train Linda, my wife, as a wrestler, and had given her a few elementary lessons. When we arrived at a place called Blaenau Ffestiniog, Orig was told that one of his female wrestlers couldn't turn up, so he suggested that Linda step in. I tried reasoning with him that she was not ready, but what was the point? So, in stepped Linda, completely raw, up against a five-foot nine-inch opponent, with a 46-inch bust. Linda was superb, and continued to wrestle for the remainder of the tour – and stole all my thunder. And that really pissed me off – but then she always has got the better of me!

Above all else, Orig was a character – a pleasant rogue and a good friend.

JOHNNY 'RASPUTIN' HOWARD

I've been in more scrapes and tight corners with Orig, or 'Bandit – the last of the Magnificent Seven' as I used to call him – than with any other man I've known. I've been lost in snowdrifts on the Welsh mountains, had to run for my life in Pakistan and, as for Ireland, I don't know how we survived. He'd take us to some of the remotest Irish villages where there were genuinely strong young men who were used to working on farms and handling heavy machinery and large animals. If this lot thought they were being taken for a ride by one of Orig's fake posters, then there would be hell to pay. Imagine what these lads could do to wrestlers who had never been outside the gym? There were some serious narrow escapes, but as long as he could have the craic in a bar after the show, all was forgiven, and usually forgotten. He was like that, the man who told me that it would be better to wrestle for him, rather than wrestle against him – in other words, for Joint Promotions.

I wrestled for him most years, since, when all is said and done, he was a man of his word – always fun, with a song or story for everywhere. What he did not tell you was that touring with him would involve babysitting Tara and sharing those duties with Haystacks. But that was part and parcel of the Orig 'thing' – it was a family, a very close-knit bond – but he was the boss!

He used to give you passes in order to travel on the Manx ferry to the Isle of Man. Administration was not Orig's forte, and I don't think in all those years he gave me the right pass. Somehow or other I was always Tina Starr. Orig would have the correct pass – the rest of us had to fend on our own. He was a strict, stiff old bugger, but we have lost a major character, and I miss those singing and shouting sessions. I've lost contact with most of the boys by now. Wrestling was my life at one stage, but no more. Yet, whenever Orig brought his shows over this way to Ireland, I would make a point of meeting up with him. That is how much this man meant to me.

DAVE FINLAY Snr

Our relationship began in the 1960s when I was doing some promotions in Ireland and Orig had his shows in Wales. Then, he came over to Ireland and used my wrestlers. He had this Celtic thing and he really loved Ireland, especially the body-building substance called Guinness, which also loosened tongues and prompted lies. It was a great relationship, because every day was a Saturday to Orig. He took my son, Dave 'Fit' Finlay, under his wing as a seventeen-year-old, and Dave started his professional career with Orig.

Orig was running summer shows on the Isle of Man and would invite us over. However, we had to travel to Liverpool to catch the ferry, some ten or twelve of us. But he'd only have one ferry ticket for us all, and we would have to form a close shuffling file and somehow dupe the ticket collector to let us on. This didn't just happen once, it happened every time. But on one occasion, he was desperate for Dave and me to wrestle for him on the Isle of Man. He even hired a private plane to fly us from Ulster. We thought we had really arrived 'big time', until we realised that it was the ferry and rail home.

I do remember a joint promotion of ours in Omagh at the height of the Irish troubles. Orig had brought over Adrian Street, and the Irish crowd thought he was English, although in fact Adrian was a very proud Welshman. The mood was threatening, and Adrian thought they were having a go at him as a flamboyant heel. Billy, my brother, was refereeing, and both of us knew that this was going to turn ugly. Suddenly, missiles were thrown at us in the ring – potatoes with razor blades in them, blocks of wood with nails – it was time for a quick exit. Adrian, meanwhile, was still winding up the crowd. We grabbed him, made for the exit, and told Adrian to make a run for it. He was still waving his arms about – with the mob giving chase. We made it to the car, which wouldn't start. I had armed myself with a broken chair leg. It was used. How we escaped only God knows. And to this day, I don't know where Orig was, but I can presume…

BRIAN DIXON

Where do I start? I was Orig's MC at the age of sixteen, and come to think of it, I am not sure he paid me when I first started working for him! We travelled everywhere, and if you wanted an education in thinking on your feet, this was it – Orig's university. I became a compère, referee, rigger and driver – a man for all reasons!

I stayed with him for about eight years, and ended up doing just about everything – the setting up, pulling down, anything you could think of. You see, apart from being a wrestler, Orig was also a raconteur, and there was nothing he enjoyed more than a session in an Irish pub. If he wasn't around, I knew where to find him.

I'd be sent to put up posters with the insulting command, "I am sending a man to do a boy's job, so don't come back with any posters." I remember telling him on one of our tours that I was ill. Back came the retort, "You've got no time to be ill," and that became our catchphrase for years.

It was a constant battle against Joint Promotions and sometimes we struggled to get venues. Unfortunately, we didn't agree on priorities. Orig, at that time, was more interested in the fight against JP than promoting and presenting our own shows. For him, it became a bitter personal vendetta with JP. He also frowned at any of our male wrestlers having any kind of association with the female wrestlers. Eventually, I decided to go on my own as a promoter, taking Mitzi, my wife, with me. That did not go down well at all – it was a strained and silent period.

Thankfully, peace was eventually restored, albeit after quite a few years. This was probably prompted by my having signed up a lot of the TV stars who had left Joint Promotions. I'd also made some progress getting television exposure. Orig also needed the top of the bill stars to keep going and he had secured wrestling coverage on the Welsh-language channel, S4C. In the end, Joint Promotions themselves were totally reliant on Big Daddy. So peace broke out between Orig and me – and since he was not the type to forgive and forget, that was a major breakthrough!

His most successful period was the launch of the 'tribute shows' – a copy of the American stars seen on television. How he got away with it, I will never know. I suspect that the shows in various corners of Wales were not deemed to be a threat to Atlanta. There is no question that he was larger than life – he would get away with some unbelievable stuff – but he was a survivor, and thankfully, a great mate and an unbelievable character. The cast can now be thrown away. There will never be another one like him.

MITZI MUELLER

I can't remember ever having a cross word with Orig in all the years we worked together. Maybe he had a soft spot for me, I don't know, because some of the others certainly didn't enjoy the same fortune.

What I do remember about those years – and it's a long time ago now – was that it was bloody hard. Sometimes I wrestled four or five nights a week, but I was the daughter of a wrestler, so I knew the scene. I began wrestling as a fourteen-year-old and back then there was no opposition, apart from the men.

We travelled in the ring van and slept in it often, and I

remember many a time having to find Irish farmers with tractors to pull us out late at night when the van got stuck in the mud. If it was a tour, then we would have shows every night, and living with the same company of wrestlers in the ring van was no picnic – more a health hazard. One night, Brian, who was refereeing with Orig at the time, accidentally trod on my hair as I was trying to get up into the ring. I had very long hair in those days, and he took more than a few clumps out. I let rip in the changing room later that night, but he ended up as my promoter and husband. There were only a few of us, and naturally wherever we went we drew a lot of attention. That was a plus, because it eventually created a lot of other openings on television for me – like parts in *Emmerdale Farm*, *Juliet Bravo* and *Minder*.

There was a fair amount of bitchiness amongst us, back-stabbing, that sort of thing. I even had my gown cut up in strips by one of my so-called fellow wrestlers. On the road shows I think Naughty Nancy Barton and I were paid £4 a night, but Orig, like all promoters wouldn't cough up until the end of the week. I remember, towards the end of one week, Nancy and I were starving and skint. We had a £1 between us and we invested that in a bag of biscuits to keep us going for two shows. How was that for a glamorous life?

But wherever we went with Orig, it was always a frantic experience – and often something had gone wrong. Somebody – always a 'w*****' in Orig's language – had let him down. And then, of course, there were the Turkish adventures. I have never been so frightened. Orig had promised female wrestling, which had never happened in Turkey before. Leyla, his other female wrestler, had missed the flight from Heathrow so we couldn't stage a female bout. When this was announced – all hell broke loose!

TINA STARR

I wanted to be a veterinary surgeon, but I had no hope of getting the qualifications. So my mum took me to see Orig, and at fourteen years of age, I became a female wrestler – the youngest in the country. I was sixteen when he took me, with a load of other girls, to wrestle in Nigeria for what was billed the world championships. He looked after me as if I were his own daughter, and my career with Orig lasted twenty-five years!

There were few other females around at the beginning, so I was thrown in with the men. In particular, I remember Mighty Chang, aka Crusher Mason and Mark 'Rollerball' Rocco. Oh yes, I was trained by the best in the business. In the ring I was ridiculously small in comparison – an Asda carrier bag compared with an airline suitcase! No insults intended, girls, but Klondyke Kate was three times the size of me!

I went to Ireland with the gang as their adopted trainee. Nobody else wanted to ride with Giant Haystacks, so they propped me up with cushions in the driving seat of Orig's Range Rover and I was given the responsibility of getting Haystacks and me to the venue. Orig wouldn't allow Haystacks to drive because he had a habit of falling asleep at the wheel. His task was to read the map and give me directions. He was hopeless! He'd be droning on about something, and the next thing you knew, he was fast asleep. Inevitably we got lost, about a hundred miles from where we should have been and never made the performance. Orig's response? It was expletive Irish mist!

TONY FRANCIS
I first met Orig when he booked me to appear at Rhyl Town Hall on the recommendation of Bobby Barron in Blackpool. Orig insisted on calling Bobby 'Dodgy Dave Shilitoe'. The atmosphere in Rhyl was amazing. Orig had a flair for creating excitement and buzz wherever he staged shows. The thing I remember most from that first meeting was that he paid me more than any other of the promoters from that era. He also took me on a tour of the Middle East, because I wasn't a 'George'! I have yet to decipher what that meant, though I suspect I know. Orig was a man amongst men, well respected and popular with most of the boys, which says a great deal when talking about a promoter in the wrestling business.

KLONDYKE KATE

He kept calling himself the 'prince of Wales'. He didn't have to, since that is what he was to us. Some twenty-five years and 15,000 fights ago, he told me I wouldn't make a wrestler as long as I had a hole in my a***! That was him – he had a cutting edge to his humour. He was witty, worried, and the very best man to have around you. I loved him to bits! Maybe that was because he had been a football manager and team player, I don't know. But he expected you to give in return what he gave to you. I was fourteen years old when I convinced Bobby Barron in Blackpool that I was serious about my chosen career. I also went to the famous Rhyl garage school to be trained by Orig and 'Crusher' Mason, and Orig looked after me from then on, even letting me stay in one of his Rhyl flats. Mind you, we fell out over a thousand times, and he'd rant, rave and blaspheme for a while, but in half an hour he'd completely forgotten what the row had been about.

Orig was exceptionally kind – sometimes I was allowed to take my young boy on his European road shows and then he'd give me some pocket money for the kids. Though I'd protest that I wasn't hard up at all, he was insistent – children mattered a great deal to him.

I was frightened to approach him at one stage. I told him I was leaving wrestling, to study for some GCSEs. I thought I would be in for a right old Welsh tirade. But nothing could have pleased him more, since he respected people who wanted to better themselves. I couldn't believe his encouragement, and I can't think of another promoter who would have given his blessing to such news. He respected knowledge, and had an insatiable memory for words and poetry.

What Orig did, not only for me, but for Tina, Rusty Blair and the Cherokee Princess was to give us the best grounding possible. We were trained and coached but he would not expose us to the ring until he thought we were ready. He looked after us. But that sort or training and preparation does not happen today. Orig was old school. A rough Welsh diamond perhaps, but an incredible character, and I owe so much to him. I remember him warning me once, "If I find out that you are involved in anything dodgy, you won't be working for me." This, from Orig, was priceless!

I remember staying in a hotel in north Wales after a show, and a Welsh male voice choir turned up and started singing in Welsh. Orig was in his element, but then Mark 'Rollerball' Rocco started singing some English 'ditty'. Orig was incensed, and literally kicked Rocco out of the room. Not once, but several times, the big star from Madison Square Gardens was given the Orig boot!

If you were down, it was, "Get a drink down you, girl". And the drink was a major part of the Orig road show psychology. I miss all that now, or do I? There are some characters I don't miss. Les Kellet was one. He did speak to me, but he was pretty horrible. There are tales of what he would do to complete strangers with those hands of his. And he had a vile temper. But people queued to see him wrestle. My favourite was Steve Logan – great to look at, and a gentleman. Not many of those around now.

The industry has changed. Youngsters, after a few fights and minimal training, call themselves promoters, and they mimic the stunts they have seen on WWE television. It depresses me and accidents will happen nowadays, because promoters do not care. When you have been groomed around the Rollerballs, St Clairs, Finlays, Masons and Nultys of the wrestling world, you know how much work you have to put in to make it happen. Orig taught me that – my very own prince of Wales.

PETER NULTY

In his wrestling days, Orig was one of the best villains in the business, and could make any blue-eyed youngster look good. But he did have a mean streak. Deep down he really liked to hurt people. If you were with him in the ring and he had you down, you had to be very careful as you got up off the canvas, as he might kick you in the ribs. His foot stomps to the chest were like being hit by a cement block. After the first one you had to grab his foot or you would get another one. But one night, the tables were turned on him. He was on with Tony St Clair and using his full repertoire of dodgy tactics. After a few rounds Tony was threatening to chin him. Orig wouldn't listen, moved forward a little and Tony threw a punch which caught him full force on his chin. He went down like a ton of bricks. The expression on his face was priceless. Total shock! Not one of us could keep a straight face.

Orig has played a big part in my life for the past thirty years. We spoke on the phone almost every day, and sometimes several times a day. He liked to portray himself as the hard, fighting man, but underneath the ruthless exterior was a gentle man with a heart of gold. He was the kindest, most generous man I ever met. I didn't believe the terrible news of his death when I first heard it, and I still find it hard to believe now. I idolised the man. He was like a brother to me, and I will miss him terribly.

He was many things during his long career. He was a footballer, wrestler, promoter, author, after-dinner speaker, television presenter – the list goes on. And everything he did revolved around his wife Wendy and his daughter Tara. They always came first. He was so proud of Tara and her achievements, but never told her. That was his way. He never gave anyone praise. He didn't think it was a good idea. He adored Wendy and would have been lost without her. Her love and dedication throughout their time together, and her great patience in his later years when he wasn't so mobile, was unsurpassed.

Over five hundred people attended his funeral. Wrestlers from past and present mingled together to show their love and affection for the man who had touched all their hearts in one way or another over the years. Old friends who hadn't seen each other for many years made promises to keep in touch.

Orig never had any interest in wrestling reunions but he would have loved the get-together at the hotel after the funeral. Friends from all walks of life gathered to celebrate his life, as his favourite music, the Irish rebel songs, were blasted out. I know he was watching from above with his old pal Dave Stalford, a pint of Guinness in his hand and enjoying every bit of it. While I was sitting in the chapel during the service I couldn't help imagining him sitting behind a small table by the door, and saying to me, "I told you this would be a good house!"

Orig, you were a legend, especially to me. It was an honour to have known you, and to have called you my friend.

TONY St CLAIR

I remember the night that Peter has just mentioned. One of his wrestlers had failed to turn up, so Orig took his place. I don't think he had wrestled for about five years, so we agreed on a course of action – more sparring than wrestling. Whereas Orig was a great showman – one of the best – as a wrestler he wasn't technically brilliant. Suddenly, he started to play every dirty kick and punch in the book. I wasn't having that, so I decked him. I can recall his words to me, sitting on the floor with a puzzled look, "You can't do that to me! I am the f****** promoter." We laughed for days.

I think it was 1972 when we first met, in a pub run by another Welsh wrestler and showman, Roy Bull Davies. We got on like a house on fire from day one, maybe because we were both the rebellious type. I was with Joint Promotions then, and one of their main people. "You stay there, Tony," Orig said, "Stay on the television and make the most of it." But we kept in touch and about ten years later, I'd had enough of the Big Daddy thing with JP and phoned Orig and Brian Dixon, who had already signed up Mighty John Quinn, Wayne Bridge and Dave 'Boy' Taylor. "Yes," Orig said, "you can join us, but you have got to bring your British heavyweight championship belt with you – that is a condition!" I did that, though JP and Crabtree, rather pettily, created another title.

Let me tell you that being on the road with Orig was one of the happiest and funniest times of my life. There were no stars: we were ring crew one minute, bodyguards to Wendy and Tara the next, sold tickets, and then wrestled. We went everywhere: Sudan, Saudi Arabia, Oman and Zimbabwe – where we dined with Robert Mugabe. I wish I could have heard what the Welsh prince said to Mugabe and his wife! But it was in Ireland where Orig excelled and came to life! Those road trips in the bus from one village to another, via a pub or two, were fantastic and unbelievable times. Could he talk? He could talk you into submission, which is probably how he negotiated contracts!

He may have sacked me once or twice, for not turning up for his shows in Llandudno, but what I remember most about him was his genuine kindness, not only to me, but to my late son – and also his interest in Ryan, my grandson, now a Newcastle United player. Orig looked after his people, and in what was sometimes a brutal and challenging life, he was a genuine friend.

MIGHTY JOHN QUINN

While working in England for Max Crabtree of Joint Promotions, I'd heard through the wrestling grapevine that Orig Williams, the Welsh promoter, wanted me to contact him, and the word was that he wanted me to join his stable. We arranged to meet, at my place, after a show in Chester. I was living in a motor home. In strode El Bandito in his pin-striped suit, looking like some gangster from the Al Capone era, with the confidence and self-assurance of 'The Godfather'.

I won't forget his first words. "Hello, I'm Orig Williams, the best damn promoter in the world, and I have come to make you an offer you can't refuse." My wife and I looked at each other thinking, "Wow! What an entrance." That was the beginning of an awesome relationship between us, both on a professional and personal level. We became great friends and I can truly say that this was a man that I really came to love.

Needless to say I went to work for Orig, and the rest is history. But allow me to go back to that first meeting, because it ended as dramatically as it had started. Orig tossed down a bag full of bills and said, "Here is a thousand pounds on good faith. If you don't make what I promise you, it is yours to keep – no questions asked. But if you fill the houses, as I am sure you will, then I get it back." We had a deal!

A couple of years later, my wife and I were expecting our second child. We were at Orig and Wendy's home in Rhyl for dinner. Orig was pouring the wine as we took our seats around the dining table. "So, have you decided on any names yet?" he asked. We mentioned a few we had decided upon if it was another boy, but couldn't agree on a girl's name. "Leave it to Orig," he said. After a pause, "Now then John, you like your wine, and I know you will like this one, so why not call her after the wine – Chianti Ruffino?" My wife and I looked at each other, and knew at once that that was the name. Our beautiful daughter was born and was named Chianti Maria Quinn and I'm delighted that she also came to know and love Orig and Wendy.

EDDIE ROSE

I first worked for Orig in the late 1960s and was immediately impressed by his warmth, enthusiasm, sense of fun and that naughty grin. I was new to professional wrestling and Orig gave me great encouragement – and he always paid quite well. I worked at many of his venues in Wales and the north of England, Llandudno, wet Tuesdays at Bethesda, Chorley, Preston and many other towns. My favourite though was Rhyl Town Hall. I took my nine-year-old son Chris to Rhyl and as soon as we walked into the changing room, Orig took charge and introduced him to all the wrestlers. I remember my son being particularly impressed by Crusher Mason. Orig could not do enough for my boy and both Chris and I loved him for that.

Ian 'Mad Dog' Wilson sometimes partnered me in the first bout of the evening on these nights. As we went into the ring one night, Orig stepped forward to tell us to do the full eight-round draw, and to be prepared for another round if we had the signal that the next bout had not arrived. So we did it – nine rounds – and came out of the ring, sweaty and absolutely out on our feet, but happy that we had helped out. We got back to the changing room to be greeted by all the boys in fits of laughter, including the next bout, who had been there for half an hour.

And against the same opponent, at a big hotel in Llandudno, I got caught in the first round by a flying knee that forced my teeth through my bottom lip. There was blood everywhere. Orig, concerned for my health and well-being, or so I thought, dashed to ringside. "Don't swallow any blood," he ordered, "just have a drink of water and dribble the blood out slowly." The blood dribbled for the next three rounds, until common sense prevailed and I had to retire. The audience was electrified by all of this – and Orig was as pleased as punch. I had to have five stitches.

I was a run-of-the-mill wrestler, but I can say that whether you were top of the bill or a journeyman, Orig looked after you.

His society was classless. He was a great promoter in more sense than one, good fun, with that giveaway wolfish grin.

JOHNNY SAINT

I knew Orig for the best part of fifty years. He was with a fellow promoter called Jack Jefferson to begin with. Orig was what you would call a 'man's man'. He believed what he said, or at least made you think he believed it. He didn't suffer fools gladly, and his schemes were always inventive, to say the least. But he didn't let you down, and I know how hard he worked to make things happen. I was proud to be a part of his operation, it was always entertaining – to say the least. His company was excellent, always engaging, and having him on my doorstep was certainly an asset.

SAM BETTS

I used to fight as Dwight J Ingleburgh who came from New Jersey in the States, although I was really from Barnsley. I travelled everywhere with Orig, and fought some of the best, including the Bholu Brothers in Pakistan.

Orig certainly had a lot of bottle; nothing seemed to faze him, although I suspect he had more scrapes than he cared to admit. But with the wrestlers, he was an honest promoter, and he did look after you – which wasn't always the case with some of them! It would have been a much tougher life without him. And he was witty, with a quick phrase for every occasion.

I remember him refereeing a match in Pakistan, where I was up against Goga – one of the Bholu brothers. I was on the mat, but doing fairly well in front of a 72,000 fanatically partisan Pakistani crowd. Up steps Orig in the third round and whispers, "Sam, you must not beat this man, otherwise we will not get out of here alive."

I travelled with Klondyke Bill and Ski Hi Lee, a real wrestling cocktail. But it was his UK shows that were a real test of stamina. Sometimes we would fight every night of the week, doubling up as masked men some nights. It could be Isle of Man, Bangor or Lancashire; he had an extraordinary amount of energy, and was tough with it.

EDDIE HAMILL – THE AMAZING KUNG FU

After working with and knowing Orig for some fifty years, it was only at his funeral I found out how old he was! Not one of us knew, since he would never let you see his passport. He probably had other secrets as well, a locker-full!

I had joined Orig at Rhyl when the troubles started in Northern Ireland. It was quite an apprenticeship: I was doorman at his nightclub, ring crew, wrestler and we would travel the length and breadth of the country. He'd have posters made with huge letters – KELLET, PALLO, McMANUS – all the big TV names, but if you looked closely below, in fine print, their Christian names were Len, John and Mark. He was like every promoter, always scheming and dodging for the extra buck.

Some of his schemes were plain daft! The promoters in those days were given nicknames by the wrestlers – 'Tricky', 'Dodgy' and 'Bandit' (Orig) – so that will give you some idea of their hard-earned reputations! Orig was a 100 per cent showman – he had the ability to wind up any audience, but it did help to have some of the game's most talented characters around.

Some of the scrapes we got into were unbelievable, and thank God we were operating in a pre-politically correct time. We travelled to Turkey, Zimbabwe and the Sudan, and wherever you went, there was always a crisis, and if not, Orig would create one. He was larger than life, and it was great fun.

By now I have had two heart operations, and my legs have gone. All my injuries are because of wrestling, but I would do it all over again – but the likes of Orig Williams and his ways of operating could never be repeated, he'd be arrested!

DAFYDD HYWEL – ACTOR

He was an extraordinary Welshman. He may have been a wrestler, promoter and footballer – but he could shame many an academic with his knowledge of Welsh culture, and poetry in particular. He had his favourite Welsh poets – Cynan, Dafydd ap Gwilym, T H Parry-Williams, Goronwy Owen – and Orig could recite their works, poem after poem. And believe you me, the works of these poets are not easy to memorise. I'm sure that reciting them on those long journeys to and from the shows kept him awake. And he had a fascination for Irish culture, which Haystacks would have appreciated. Orig was a man of the people – no frills, no protocol, just plain Orig. He was great friend to many, and that affection was returned.

GEORGE BURGESS – JAMAICA KID

The money wasn't good, but it was a living. Orig's company was always entertaining – and that goes for the thirty years I knew and travelled with him. I saw the world with Orig, the Middle East, India, Pakistan, and every single village in Scotland, Ireland and his beloved Wales.

We got on famously. I didn't drink, though most of the boys did, and Orig wouldn't pass the opportunity of a pint either. Sometimes, through drink, there were problems with some of the wrestlers, but Orig always looked after me. He would take me aside, and if there was an issue we would talk about it, and he would sort it out. At the time, some of the big names didn't appreciate what he did for them, and certainly didn't know how he had to operate to survive. Wendy and Orig were a top team – and I loved them both.

We were forever distributing flyers, especially in Ireland. Occasionally we would be spotted at 2a.m. or 3a.m. in the morning in the middle of the Irish countryside – a black man with a white van, placing posters everywhere. The police would be called but, by the time they arrived, Wendy would be driving, and Orig and I would be hiding underneath the ring inside the van!

We had some scrapes, especially with a goat tied to a bed in Pakistan – but I know that story has done the rounds several times in the wrestling world. We shared bedrooms infested with rats, mice and cockroaches in India and Pakistan. We ate baked beans from tins in such places because you couldn't trust the food. He became suspicious of one meal he had ordered. He wanted lamb, but it didn't taste right. When he was told he was eating goat – he threw up!

I miss him greatly. He was one of the characters – the kind of loyal character that wrestling lacks these days.

ANDREW BLACKWELL – 'BLACKIE'

I was with him for twenty years – from my very first bout, when a bloke head-butted me and I lost my teeth, and Orig gave me £40 to have them repaired, until the day I retired from the ring. Sometimes we would do between twelve and fifteen shows a week, and they could be in Rhyl one night, the Isle of Man the next and then on to Great Yarmouth.

He was a great promoter and a fantastic friend. Naturally, he would sack me on a regular basis – but then he sacked everyone but never bore grudges. What I really admired about him was his brain. He loved to talk with people who knew about a subject he didn't. On our travels, when mobile phones and iPods started to become fashionable, he wouldn't have them in the van, simply because they destroyed conversation. The man's knowledge was extraordinary, and his inventive approach to promotions was legendary. I remember one free-for-all, with a few of us in the ring and one of the wrestlers was catapulted out. His head was cracked, with blood pouring everywhere. "Blackie!" came the instruction, "put a towel round his head. We don't want people to see that."

RAYMOND 'COMMANDO' JONES – NANTLLE VALE FC

As a player-manager, he would insist on having the last word. But then he insisted on having the last word in every situation. We were not so much a football team at Nantlle, more a squad of storm troopers. We did have a reputation as being hard, and there was only one man responsible for that.

I remember the dressing room before a game against Rhyl, who had an excellent centre-forward by the name of Johnny Jones. He was, however, a 'niggler', known for the odd sly kick. Orig wanted to move me from centre-half to left-back and I couldn't understand why. "Listen, Commando, that boy will give you a kicking, you will lose your temper, and we will be a man down. So I will play centre-half, and that is final."

The game kicked off. Jones, the danger man, passed to his inside-left who rolled the ball back to the wing-half. He, in turn, chipped a high ball into our penalty area. But as we turned to defend, there was Johnny Jones lying motionless on the floor, completely out for the count. The game was seconds old. We knew what had happened, the referee knew what had happened, but no one had seen what had happened. Orig's face gave nothing away.

JAMES MASON

I was obsessed with wrestling from a very young age, so when I joined Brian Dixon as a fourteen-year-old wrestler I thought I had arrived! That was, of course, merely the start, but I do remember my first encounter. It was in Ireland, in the company of Drew McDonald and Tony St Clair. I attempted to keep up with the drinking pace, which was of Olympic standard! Naturally I failed, and had to be put to bed. I suffered the consequences and had my eyebrows shaven whilst I was asleep.

Working with Orig was different from any other promoter. First, I had to endure his daily four-letter references to me being an 'English' something or other – it was never complimentary. I was also told that he didn't trust a man who didn't drink. I think I had a Coke in my hand at the time. He then told me that my wrestling name was boring. He didn't like the actor James Mason, so with Orig I became Jesse James. El Bandito had a thing about bandits and crooks.

But he did treat me and the others as human beings, and ultimately, if you had passed the bar-room test, as friends. That was the thing about Orig's road show. There were no stars, and everybody was part of the family team. I was surrounded by my idols, but it didn't matter, there was no question as to who was the boss. We would all sit around for hours having fun, telling terrible lies – it was a truly enjoyable time.

The big stars really looked forward to the Orig tours, especially Ireland, because they were totally different. We could all show heavily stamped passports, boasting that we had travelled the world, but the Quinns and St Clairs of this world would never say no to a week of Orig sessions in Ireland.

I still wrestle a bit, and have my own ring for hire, but these days, I mainly do security work. There's not much good wrestling around these days. Why do it? I've often been asked that. It is the twenty or so minutes that you are in the ring. You are the centre of attention, and that is a buzz! I watched the wrestlers as a kid and I was fortunate to wrestle, and the thrill will never leave me. I worked for Orig for some six years, travelling all over the place, and won the Welsh heavyweight title in Harlech! A f****** Englishman! I'm surprised I got out of the country.

IDRIS WYN EVANS – 'TARW NEFYN', NANTLLE VALE FC

We played together at Pwllheli, Penmaenmawr and Nantlle Vale. The period in which Orig was player-manager at Nantlle Vale was one of the most notorious in the Welsh game. Orig was always being disciplined and appearing before various governing bodies. But he was quite a good attorney. I remember at one disciplinary meeting, where the referee's report accused Orig of kicking an opponent's ankle but the linesman said it was a blow to the knee. That was enough for Orig. He denied both charges and said it was somewhere between the two. He got off!

Being around Nantlle was so much fun, never a dull moment. Orig's half-time talks were always to do with *Saeson* – the English. And if we had played a lacklustre first half, his call to battle was something else. One game had to be abandoned because our opponents, Llandudno, were reduced to seven men.

But he looked after us, and often out of his own pocket. He once flew from France to be on the field at Nantlle on the Saturday afternoon. Orig would be incensed when people called us a dirty side, claiming instead that we were 'hard but fair'. But he also knew that Nantlle's notoriety would attract the press boys, and I think Nantlle had more coverage than the rest of league put together. That pleased Orig. Notoriety was the name of game.

DAVE 'FIT' FINLAY

I wrestled for Orig as a fourteen-year-old teenager, when I was on holiday in Rhyl, and he treated me like a son. My father ran wrestling shows in Ireland, but because of the troubles no one would come to Ireland – except Orig.

He was larger than life: bold, loud, but inside he was a generous, caring, warm-hearted man. He and Wendy took care of my family and me, and I owe them so much.

Orig wanted me to go to the United States, but I resisted. He called me everything. "Finlay," he said, in that awesome Welsh accent of his, "I have a crystal ball. You need to go to the USA. If you don't, I am going to stick my crystal ball where the sun doesn't shine." Or words to that effect. I did eventually go, and the rest is history.

But in those days, on the road, it was great fun. We were one big happy family with Orig and Wendy at the head of it. I had the pleasure of babysitting Tara as well, constantly tormenting her, and telling her she should marry me.

I wrestled Orig many times. One night he challenged me. He bet me £50 that I could not pick him up and slam me. Now it was well known that Orig was never keen on leaving the ground. But I took the bet, and halfway through the tag match, I scooped him up to slam him. Orig was airborne, but shouting, "Finlay! Put me down, or you'll never wrestle for me again, and I will tell your father!" I put him down, and told him he owed me £50. He refused to pay me, saying I hadn't slammed him. That was Orig. I owe those two so much, and it was a journey I am glad and proud to have experienced.

Also from Y Lolfa:

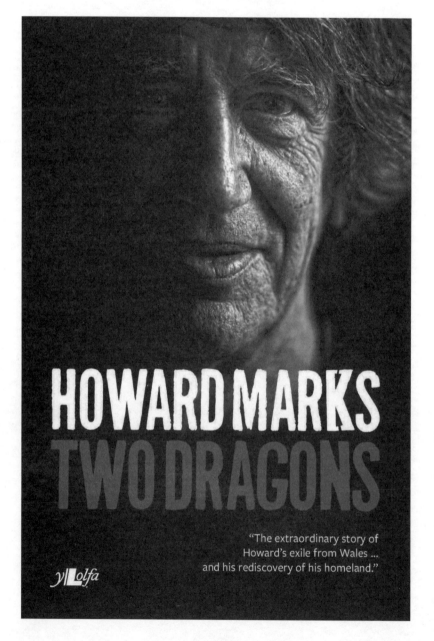

HOWARD MARKS
TWO DRAGONS

"The extraordinary story of Howard's exile from Wales ... and his rediscovery of his homeland."

yLolfa

£7.95

* Published November 2010

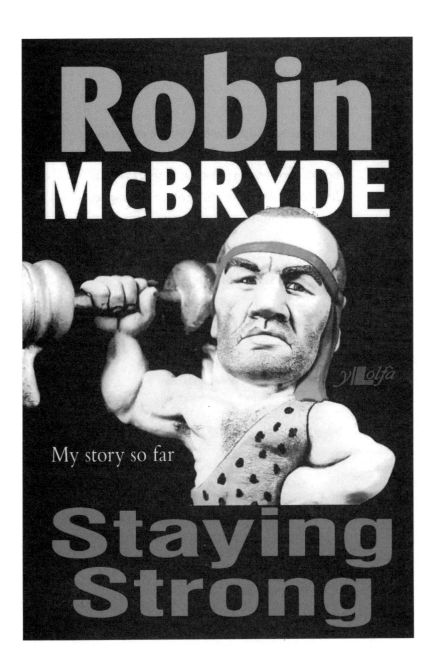

Robin
McBRYDE

My story so far

Staying
Strong

£9.95

El Bandito is just one of a whole range of
publications from Y Lolfa. For a full list of
books currently in print, send now for your
free copy of our new full-colour catalogue.
Or simply surf into our website

www.ylolfa.com

for secure on-line ordering.

TALYBONT CEREDIGION CYMRU SY24 5HE
e-mail ylolfa@ylolfa.com
website www.ylolfa.com
phone (01970) 832 304
fax 832 782